Praise f

My Love Affair

"*Doves Fly in My Heart* is part personal mystical adventure story and part wise cultural guide. Lisa's love affair with Peru is infectious and her straight talk, admirable. If you plan to visit Peru, this is a book that will serve both your spiritual curiosity and your practical needs."

-- Joan Parisi Wilcox, author of *Masters of the Living Energy: The Mystical World of the Q'ero of Peru*

****

"Lisa's love for Peru and its people shine through in this wonderful book! I love how she weaves her experience and stories with the spiritual teachings of the people of the high Andes. This book is an offering at the highest level. Lisa's life experience will leave you with a guide to navigate the portal of the unknown worlds of the Peruvian spirit work."

-- Beverley Gray, author of *Boreal Herbalist*

****

"Lisa McClendon Sims opens to the door of her heart -- with intelligence, wonder and realism -- to bring us the magic and people of the Peruvian high country. Doves Fly in My Heart offers the full-spectrum of a seeker's experience. It's the challenge and euphoria of adjusting to a new culture, and it's the authentic story of a person coming face-to-face with her spiritual core."

-- Jeremy A. Hillpot, writer and founder of the *Cusco Writer's Guild*

Doves Fly in My Heart

My Love Affair with Peru

(Urpichay Sonqochay)

By Lisa McClendon Sims

www.SpiritualJourneysPeru.com
DovesFlyInMyHeart@gmail.com

Cover Design by Dennis E. McClendon

ISBN-13: 978-1514818039
ISBN-10: 1514818035

The beautiful young man with brown skin and a pointed hat, dripping in tiny white beads and brightly colored tassels, put his hand on his heart and bowed slightly. With his eyes closed he said, "Urpichay sonqochay."

"Doves fly in my heart" is the way he told me "thank you."

Table of Contents

Acknowledgements

Thank you to the Apus (especially Wamanlipa), Pachamama and all of the people of Peru for making this story and my life in Peru possible.

Thank you to Juan & Rebeca Quispe, their extended family, and all of the Q'ero masters who have touched and enhanced my life in so many ways. Thank you to my teachers, Elizabeth Jenkins and Joan Parisi Wilcox.

A huge thank you to The Cusco Writer's Guild who inspired and supported me throughout the entire process of writing this book– especially Ocean Malandra, Jeremy Hillpot, Cesar Moran Cahusac, Jahanshah "JJ" Javid and to the magnificent and patient Michelle Tupy for her infinite patience and guidance. Without you, Michelle, this book would not exist. Thank you to Dennis E. McClendon the book cover design.

Thank you to the many people who helped to edit, refine and proofread: Diana Waldron, Emma Bussett-Lovall, Liza Callen, Beverly Wakefield, Margarita Reinaga, Luz Azpilcueta, Patricia Anaya, Danise Maiqui, David Walton, Ellyn Jameson, Denise Chastain, Maureen Santucci and Beverley Gray.

Thank you to the many, many people who helped me live these stories, especially Roger Meinke, Lesley Myburgh, Elizabeth Jenkins, Seti Gershberg, Segundo Valverde Aguilar, David Moore, Kush, Danni Jade, Nelly Rivera, Ingrid Zimmermann, and my gorgeous children, Melissa and Jesse Sims.

Thank you to those of you who encouraged me for years to write: Ralph Hume, Mary Bryant, Carolyn Rilling, and Joey Curtin. You have no idea how much your words of encouragement made a difference in my life and influenced this book. I have held your words in my heart, and they have given me strength over the years.

Author's Note on Language

Many of the words in this story come from the Quechua language, the language of the ancient Inka, which is still very much alive in many parts of South America. There is a glossary of these words at the back of this book for your convenience. Quechua was not a written language until the Spanish came in the 1500s, consequently, today you will find many different spellings for words. The current trend is to spell things phonetically, though you will frequently find the Spanish influence in some of the words. There are also sounds in Quechua which the English/Roman alphabet doesn't have letters for—particularly a click, or slight pause in the middle of the word which is usually indicated by an apostrophe. The sound of the letters Q and K, are frequently replaced with CC which has a sharper sound than those letters alone.

For example, the ancient Inka capital of Peru in English is spelled *Cuzco*. In Spanish it is spelled *Cusco*, and in Quechua, it is spelled *Qosqo,* which translates to "navel." In the Inka cosmology, Qosqo was the place where our world connected to Mother Earth, and was the center of the Inka universe.

Q'eros, which has a click with the *Q* and a slight pause after the apostrophe, is sometimes seen as being spelled *Queros*, using the English rule where *q* is always followed by a *u*, which in fact, is not a correct pronunciation at all.

The Spanish assigned *hu* to what is also frequently written with a *w*. For instance, one of the high mountains in Cusco is called *Saqsaywaman*, but you will also you see it spelled *Sacsayhuaman*.

While reading this book, please don't get caught up in the spelling of things. I repeat: Quechua was not a written language—the rules don't apply here.

I use the term *shaman* rather loosely. The word shaman originated from Siberia but is generally accepted in use when talking about people who walk between the worlds of the reality we accept as "normal" and alternate realities or altered states of consciousness. When talking about shamans that work with a specific path, I use that term specifically, for example, Paqos, Pampamisayoqs, Ayahuasqeros, and Wachumeras.

In Spanish, gender is frequently shown by whether a word ends in "a" which is generally feminine, or by an "o," which is usually masculine. When you see my words ending in "o/a," as in "gringo/a," I am referring to that description in general, without attaching a specific gender to it.

In Peru, we choose to use the word "gringa" with affection. "Gringo/a", as used here refers to a white person, usually from North America or Europe, but also Australia or South Africa. My friends and I refer to ourselves and each other as "gringas/os," to differentiate that we are talking specifically about ourselves culturally. Most Peruvians would not dream of calling us "gringas," as it can have a derogatory connotation. I frequently refer to myself as a *Gringa Cusqueña* to which the Peruvians either laugh with embarrassment at my audacity or gently correct me.

Preface

I remember the exact day I was bitten by the travel bug. I must've been eight or nine years old. It was in the 1960s, and my father was a press officer in the U.S. Air Force. He was frequently sent to countries where the threat of war was high or war was in progress, and these places were deemed unsafe to bring his family. So he went away for weeks, sometimes months at a time, usually to Africa or the Middle East. When he came home he always brought my sister and me a doll in native dress and coins or currency from the country where he had been. We had quite a collection.

One day I received a postcard of a camel from my father; I think he was in Jordan at the time. There was nothing on the postcard except the camel, the sand it was standing on, and the blue sky in the background. The camel was looking directly at the camera. I held that postcard in my little hands and I said, "I'm going to go see that camel one day." And I meant it. It did take a couple of decades, but eventually, when I was 4 months pregnant with my first child, my husband and I said, "This is it! We won't be traveling like this for a while with a baby, let's make this trip a good one!" I was atop a camel riding around the pyramids in Egypt. Thank you, Dad.

My first big trip was to Europe when I was 18 years old. I thought it was going to be "The Trip of a Lifetime," but little did I know the effect that wanderlust would have on me. Europe was everything that Tampa, Florida was NOT at that time. There was a great big world out there, and I wanted to experience it all! I called it my "Lust for Life," after one of Van Gogh's paintings.

I moved to London by myself when I was 20 years old. I knew no one there, and I had parted with almost everything I owned, saved up $2,000 and managed to finagle a work permit. My plan was to stay there as long as my money would last. I loved living in London; it was so cosmopolitan and so "Big City." I was able to live on the money I made there by living in a "bedsit," which was a small room approximately the size of a jail cell, in a big four-story house with shared kitchen and bathrooms. ("Well," I told myself, "at least it is easy to heat!")

I lived in Chelsea and Kensington and worked on the fashionable Kings Road at the height of the punk era, which attracted all kinds of characters and celebrities. I loved it! I worked in a store selling 1940's American "Retro" clothing, and my collection of beaded blouses and sweaters with padded shoulders was top of the line. At the end of one year, I still had my $2,000, and I decided it was time to go see more of Europe.

Over the next years I traveled to many places—back to Europe with a visit to Russia (which was still the USSR at the time), Northern Africa, a few different places in Asia, much of the Caribbean and Central America, and a couple of countries in South America. Whenever I had the money and time, that was how I spent it—traveling. I lived in San Francisco for 4 years and moved back to Tampa when my mother became ill.

Peru was never on my radar. I'm not altogether sure why. I imagine the terrorist activity of the Shining Path had an influence in this. It just seemed so far, so foreign, and possibly dangerous. Plus my Spanish wasn't that good yet.

On my tour to the USSR in 1982, I met the man whom I would eventually marry four years later. He was English and charming, and I found myself living in England again. We lived in Oxford for five years and had two babies before moving back to the United States. All of our travels during that period were pretty much back and forth over "The Pond" (as the English like to refer to the Atlantic Ocean) visiting our families. My husband and I separated in 2003, and I found myself with the freedom to take up my passion for travel again.

I always had an interest in spirituality. My family was not religious, but I was always encouraged to be open to different faiths. Conformity and dogma have never really been my strong suits. Remember that box on our report cards from school when we were little that said "doesn't take direction well"? I recall that box being checked off on my report card on more than one occasion. So in my mid-20s, I became interested in the teachings of the indigenous cultures of the Americas, less structured and more nature-based and mystical. I devoured entire libraries written by Carlos Castaneda and Lynne Andrews amongst others. I dabbled in the teachings of many other belief systems as well, but they always struck me as paths that told you exactly how to live your life, full of rules and regulations. Many had severe consequences if you strayed from their doctrine, rather than calling on you to see life as the mystery to be experienced that I felt it was, and allowing you to come to your own conclusions.

Getting married and having children changed my focus dramatically. While living in England, I became pretty immersed in the Complementary Medicines there which seemed to fulfill my need for exploring alternative ways of thinking. As my young children started growing up, I felt the need to offer some sort of spiritual path to them to give them a value base to work with in their lives. Metaphysics and quantum physics were really appealing to me at the time, but I was having trouble finding a group that resonated well with me. When my father died in 2002, I was reacquainted with a dear friend who pointed me in the direction of a metaphysical spiritual center which I found fit me just like a hand in glove, and I was "home." I was hungry for it, and with my marriage apparently dissolving, it gave me the strength and support I desperately needed to get through the next difficult years.

How wonderful it was to have people in my life who wanted my company and loved me because of who I was, not just because I was somebody's neighbor or co-worker or wife or mother or relative. Wife-dom and motherhood had swallowed me, and I didn't even know who I was anymore.

I thought I could do this, take on these roles and change who I was—I mean, hadn't I always been successful at everything I had ever done before? Here I was in my 40's, and I had done everything society had told me would make me happy and successful, but I was not happy at all. My soul was shriveling, and it was killing me. One day my Spirit snatched me by the hair and said, "Enough!! I need to be expressed! I have been shoved up in the attic for too long! You have given away your power. Stand up and reclaim it, or you will die the way your mother did—way too early!"

One Sunday, one of the ministers of the spiritual center came to me with a black and white photocopy of a tour she was organizing to Peru. The moment that paper touched my hand, it was like I'd gotten a mega-hit! I have always been lucky in that I get really clear guidance at pivotal times in my life on what is right for me in my life path, more so when I meditate. So I was going to Peru and that's all there was to it! I had to take out a home equity loan on my townhouse to pay for it and a friend came to stay with my kids for the 11 days I would be gone. Our organizer had been to Peru before, spoke Spanish, and I felt safe going with her. That was in November 2005 and my life has never been the same since.

This is the story of my love affair with Peru.

Part 1

My Personal Journey

Love at First Sight

We stood quietly in the darkened cave, waiting to see what would happen. The walls of the cave were damp, and we could hear dripping every now and then. There were mysterious ancient stone carvings in the walls—mostly altars. Deep into the cave at the back was a larger altar with three stone steps leading up to it. In the center of the altar was a shaft of light that was streaming in from an opening in the rocks high above.

It was November 2005, and there were nine of us, all women, who had come from the U.S. on a mystical journey to Peru. We had driven up the steep, unpaved, muddy roads just outside of Cusco, until we came to what appeared to be a very large mound in the countryside. There were unusual carvings on some parts of the outside of the mound which looked like they were intended to be doorways or portals of some kind—except that at the back it was solid stone and you could not pass through. They were only about 12 or 18 inches deep. There was a wide carved stairway up one side of the mound. Above Cusco, we were at nearly 12,000 feet above sea level, and the air was thin, so we walked slowly and had to stop occasionally to catch our breath.

Our guide, Jorge, walked over to a nearby walled compound and knocked on the door. The shaman opened the door and came over to join us. He did not speak English so Jorge translated for him. His name was Miguel, and he looked to be probably in his 60s.

We were told that this mound was a womb of Mother Earth. In the Andean spiritual tradition, Mother Earth is called *Pachamama* and she is a living, sentient being. We were told that this was a rebirthing chamber, and that if you were ready and chose to do so, you could be reborn in the chamber inside of this mound. We were led up the carved stone steps to a slitted opening in the mound which was meant to represent a vulva. At the opening on the right-hand side were two long snakes in the stone. We were told that the black one, which was headed into

1

the cave, was an actual petrified snake. This snake is the symbol for the *Ukhupacha*, or lower world/subconscious in the Andean tradition, and it was black because it was carrying heavy energies which it wanted to release inside the cave. Next to it was another snake which had been carved in the stone, and this one was white. It was heading out of the cave and was representative of us as we left the cave, reborn.

On the left-hand side of the opening was a partial carving of a puma. Part of it had been destroyed. The puma was representative of the middle world, the world in which we live, that the Andeans call *Kaypacha*. We were told the ancient name of this place was Amaru Machay, or Serpent Cave, though today many people called it The Temple of the Moon because when there is a full moon a bright shaft of moonlight pours in through an opening at the top of the cave, and it is frequently used for ceremonies.

"This site is not Inka. It is a pre-Inka site, and people have been using this place in a ceremonial manner for thousands of years. It is very ancient and very powerful," Jorge told us. We then quietly climbed down the stone stairs leading into the inner chamber of the mound, going very slowly and taking care not to slip on the slick stones that thousands of years of use had polished and smoothed.

Jorge stood up on the altar in the stream of light and called us up one by one. I felt a shiver go down my spine, and my skin prickled with goose bumps. My heart was pounding. He counted backwards from our age to zero, and we were instructed to go, in our minds, to that age as he counted and release any painful or negative memories from that age that we were still carrying. He said that illness was created by us holding on to heavy energies from the past and that if we release them on a regular basis as we were doing now, we would be much lighter beings. He said that these heavy energies have a place where they belong and that place is the *Ukhupacha* which we could access through caves and lakes and other places that were within the earth. He said that *Pachamama*/Mother Earth takes these energies from us as a sacred gift and transmutes them into refined energies which can be used to create something new, just as she takes the waste products from the animals and turns them into fertilizer which helps grow new life.

My husband and I had been separated for over two years. I had been unable to remove my wedding band—I just couldn't do it. To me, it was such a pure symbol—this simple gold band—and it was the last vestige of our marriage. I thought about how gold is considered divine in many cultures, pure gold being incorruptible and noncorrosive. The Inka did not use a monetary system; they used gold, which was considered to be the sweat of the sun, and silver, which was considered to be the tears of the moon, to represent the divine feminine and divine masculine.

There was really no hope of my husband and me ever getting back together, and I knew that. There was a great sadness in me and this gold band was just me clinging to the last shreds of what might have been. I never even consciously thought about wearing it; I would just look down and see it and think, "Yep, it's still there."

The moment I walked in to that cave I felt compelled to remove my wedding band. It didn't come off easily as I had gained a bit of weight since the first time I put it on, 20 years and two babies ago. But there was no doubt about it, it was coming off now. I held it in the palm of my hand, and the tears started to flow. When it was my turn, I went up the steps to the altar and stood in the shaft of light. Jorge had me hold my arms out to my sides. He then showed me one of the most powerful mantras I've ever used. I took my right hand and put it over my heart and said "Con amor" (with love), then I put my left hand over my solar plexus and said, "Sin miedo" (without fear). So simple and yet so powerful!

Jorge then started my countdown. I realized and felt most grateful that, in truth, I hadn't had a lot of fear in my life up until I got married and had children. At that time, something clicked in me and I eventually found that the responsibilities of life and marriage and motherhood were more than I could handle. I had developed a terrible case of anxiety which I had been treating with medication for years. Since I'd left my marriage things were definitely improving for me, and now, here I was standing, ringless, on an altar inside the womb of *Pachamama*, and I was ready to release it all. It was as if the walls of that cave sucked those heavy energies out of me. When I came down from the altar, I leaned back against the cool, damp wall and released the pain, the sadness, and the disappointment.

Con amor, sin miedo . . .

It was dizzying! I felt lightheaded, as if I might float away. With tears streaming down my face I took the three coca leaves that Jorge handed me and fanned them as he showed us to do. I put my intentions and desires onto the coca leaves with my breath. I connected the energy from my heart through my breath and gave my prayers to the little messenger leaves. We held the coca leaves in the palms of our hands and blew the leaves and our prayers with them out into the world. We were then told to sink deep roots from our bodies into the earth and to breathe up new clean, refined energy from *Pachamama*.

I felt so humbled and so incredibly relieved as we quietly left Amaru Machay. Several of us had tears on our cheeks and for me it was hours before they stopped.

****

From there, we drove about an hour and a half outside of Cusco through beautiful countryside where the rich, red-brown earth was worked manually by the beautiful, brown skinned campesinos and their animals, not a tractor in sight. It was springtime in the Southern Hemisphere, and the earth was coming to life with bright green plants—potatoes, quinoa, and corn. There were very few fences, spaces were wide open, and the animals in the pastures were either accompanied by a human or tethered to a stake in the ground. These people were so earthy, so connected to their land, they seemed to be a part of the earth. It fascinated me.

We ended up in a tiny village where the streets were so narrow our small bus couldn't pass through, so we got off and walked up a mountain. Miguel called the mountains "*apus*"—he said that was the name of the spirit of the mountain itself. This was a sacred place to him, and he asked that as we walked up the mountain we connect deeply through our feet with the body of this *apu*. He gave us each an open red rose and told us to connect with it through our hearts. When we got to the top of the mountain, we made a beautiful mandala with all our red roses and all our love, and we left it on the top of the mountain as a gift of our love to the *apu*. Our hearts were open.

We drove back to an archaeological site just outside of Cusco called Saqsaywaman. The ancient city of Cusco was built in the shape of a puma, the representative of the *Kaypacha*, the middle world, the world in which we live. Saqsaywaman is the head of the ethereal puma that is Cusco, considered to be one of South America's archaeological treasures, formed by three massive parallel stone ramparts which zigzag across the plateau on which it is built and which serve as the teeth of the puma. The stonework is amazing, with huge monoliths weighing as much as 200 tons each and fitted together like a jigsaw puzzle with nary a speck of mortar. The power in these stones was palpable. Miguel told us that they were from Atlantean times.

He asked us to form a half circle in front of the stones, holding hands, with the person on each end putting a flattened hand on the monoliths. He then stood in the center of the half-circle and called us into the center one-by-one where he did a cleansing ritual using flower waters and condor feathers. The condor is the representative of the *Hanaq Pacha*, the upper world in the Andean cosmology. All of these rituals, we were told, were to connect us with the sacred energies of this powerful land.

****

Miguel joined us off and on, in and out of Cusco over the next few days. He presided over several beautiful ceremonies using coca leaves and flowers and water and wind to connect us with this sacred land and to nurture the Inka seed that in the Andean cosmology is believed to be within us all. This seed had lodged itself deeply within me and was definitely taking root. I was loving the connection I was feeling. This land seemed to me to be so well-loved, and the people seemed to be so connected to it. It was so sweet, so humble and pure. I felt a strong connection with Miguel, as well, which would later make itself very apparent.

The group went to Machu Picchu, which was absolutely amazing. We spent two days wandering around this enigmatic mystical site, taking in the energies, doing ceremonies, sharing our love. We came back to Cusco for a night before heading south to see Lake Titicaca. At 12,500 feet above sea level, it is the highest navigable lake in the world. We went to see the Floating Islands of Lake Titicaca in a reed boat to see reed houses on reed islands built by people who ate the reeds. Walking on these spongey islands felt like walking on clouds. We went to an inter-dimensional doorway, where we were told whole groups of people had completely disappeared. We did a ceremony putting all of our fears on coca leaves through our breath and then burning them before taking the risk of walking into these portals. None of us disappeared, but the power of these stones was unmistakable. They were energetic vortexes, and Jorge demonstrated this by putting our incense burner full of burning aromatic woods on the vortexes, and we could watch the smoke spiral as it went up.

I had a bizarre experience there. I heard a voice behind me say, "Pick me up." I wheeled around to see from whence this voice came, and my eyes were drawn to a small stone on the ground. Well, I hadn't disappeared in the inter-dimensional doorway, but now the stones were speaking to me! I walked over to it and picked it up. What the heck was this!? I didn't know stones could speak, and I had clearly heard this—it wasn't in my head, it was actually audible! This little stone wanted to come with me!

"Oh, dear God, whatever next?!"

Feeling the Pull

That first trip to Peru had a very profound effect on me. I came back to Tampa and decided to change my life. In my meditations, I had been getting the message "Simplify your life." It was true: my life had become so incredibly complex! I had bought into the American Dream of family and children and homeownership and all the responsibilities it entails—massive mortgages, a million different types of insurance, investments, Girl Scouts, fencing lessons, soccer, school meetings, and even the drugs it takes to be able to cope with such a complex life. I had been on medication for years to help me cope with the anxiety I felt with the responsibilities of my life, marriage, children, and work. My personal needs had been denied for years and years. I had become a master at delayed gratification. By leaving my marriage, I had pulled myself out of the grave I had very nearly dug for myself, and it was definitely time now to simplify my life. In the past, I had always been so able to take on just about anything that was thrown at me, but I had recently learned that I wasn't superhuman and that there were limits to what I could handle.

Simplify your life, Lisa.

I was ready for it. I had been self-employed and/or commission-paid in various forms of real estate ever since we moved back to the U.S. in 1991. My thinking at the time was that if I were really good at what I did, I would have more control over my income and could make a lot of money. Sometimes that was true. But I also found that there were many things out of my control—market changes and trends, bosses with massive egos who decided they wanted to block me from being successful, and a myriad of other situations that had an influence on my ability to control my income while working on a commission basis.

I wanted a salaried job with set hours, something I could count on. I wanted a smaller mortgage. I was considering putting my house on the market—I mean, I was in real estate. It was a pretty decent market at the time, so I figured that I wouldn't have any problem selling. I had a very successful track record with excellent letters of recommendation from my past employers, so finding an administrative job should be no problem, right? Well, that's not the way it worked out.

I came back from my first trip to Peru in November 2005, quit the job I'd been at for the past seven years, celebrated the holidays with my family, and at the New Year, I started seeking new employment. I put my house on the market to sell and started a job hunt . . . nothing happened.

Nothing. No one called to see my house. I couldn't get a job interview for the life of me.

I had been meditating regularly and had learned that these things happen for a reason, and perhaps I needed to ask why nothing was happening. I was excellent at manifesting, and things usually happened for me pretty quickly, so why was I getting nothing?

The truth was that I longed for Peru. It tugged on my heart; it almost felt like there were hooks in my heart that were pulling me back to Peru. What was this attraction? I didn't really understand it, but the pull was very, very strong. Could it just have been that the time I spent in Peru was representative of a simpler life? Were those 11 days spent there just so attractive because it was the first time in many years I had been able to indulge myself in my own self-care without having to think of everybody else's needs? Or was there something more?

And those mountains! There was something about those mountains. I had lived half my life in Florida, which I affectionately refer to as "The Pancake State" due to its flatness— my kids used to get a thrill from just going over a high overpass in Florida. Peru was so very different from anywhere I had ever lived before. Cusco is at an elevation of over 11,000 feet above sea level, right in the heart of the Andes Mountains. It is a developing country with plenty of poverty, but there was an allure—something about it seemed to me to be much purer, much more connected. I couldn't really put my finger on it, but it was kind of like falling in love, kind of like being pulled by the tide, moved by a force that I couldn't really control.

"But I can't do this! I have a kid in high school and a kid in middle school. I have RESPONSIBILITIES here! I obviously can't go back to Peru right now. Maybe later, when the kids have grown up . . . ."

While I was in Peru the first time, I had bought just about everything in sight to bring home with me to remind me of this seemingly magical place. I had brought home some CDs of Peruvian tribal music, and at night, I would turn out the lights and have a glass of wine or two and dance around my living room alone with a rattle in my hand, and I would long for Peru. Sometimes it hurt so much it made me cry, but I'd become very good at delayed gratification. I could wait. I'd waited for years and years to meet some of my own needs after losing myself in my marriage and motherhood. My daughter would come home in the evenings to a darkened house, and her mother dancing around the living room to Peruvian tribal music, and she would say "You and your weird tribal crap...." and disappear into the safety of her bedroom.

Well, that was okay, I really was no longer the same person that my children had grown up with. That was becoming very apparent.

The answer came to me in my meditation one morning. It was very clear, it said,

"Lisa, you are doing all the right things but you are doing them for the wrong reasons. What is in your heart?"

"What is in my heart?!? Well, that is obvious. Peru is in my heart."

"Go to Peru, Lisa."

"Well, you know, that just isn't bloody convenient. I have a whacking great mortgage, and now I have a home equity loan as well. I have two kids in school, and I am unemployed."

"Just try it, Lisa."

"OH OKAY. I'll try it…." I said with great exasperation.

****

So I put my townhouse up for rent on the Internet. I got exactly one response. A couple from England sent me a check for $6,000 to rent it for three months. Much to my amazement, one of my friends said I'll take one kid and another person said I'll take the other.

More than a little stunned, I said to myself, "It looks like I'm going back to Peru . . . ." And five months after my first trip I was back there. My plan was to try to figure out a way to move there with the children.

Back to Peru

The first two weeks I enrolled in intensive Spanish language classes and spent time researching the school systems there to see if this idea was even feasible. From there I planned to spend time studying shamanism with Miguel in the compound he was building on a mountain above Cusco.

Things are not always what they appear to be. I have found that when I follow the guidance I receive through meditation that things usually turn out quite well, though not always in the way I expect them to. And this trip was going to be full of twists and turns that would change my life in ways I could never, ever have imagined.

I really enjoyed the first two weeks of Spanish classes. It was at a well-organized school that set me up in a homestay with a local family, and it even had an organized social structure with cooking and dance classes and weekend excursions to nearby archaeological sites. I didn't really know Miguel that well. I had only just met him on the trip in November and had been corresponding with him by email. He did come recommended by people that I trusted, but I didn't want to put all my eggs in one basket and just move in with an old yogi[1] who was offering to teach me about shamanism for a weekly charge. So the school was a good choice, it got me connected with other people and gave me some other options just in case this thing with Miguel didn't work out.

I met with Miguel twice while I was still in school. He was giving me suggestions on some things I might do to prepare myself for the things I would learn with him. I was just a little bit suspicious when he said, "You know, we don't have all the

---

[1] A yogi is a practitioner of yoga and broadly refers to the ascetic practitioners of meditation in a number of Indian religions including Hinduism and Buddhism.

amenities here in Peru that you're accustomed to in the United States."

After my two weeks of Spanish classes, I hired a taxi for the two kilometer drive out of Cusco and up to Miguel's house. He had made a huge amount of progress on what he called the Temple, which was a two-story roundhouse, called a "maloca," where I would be living upstairs. It was one big circular room, and he had decorated it with beautiful wall hangings that were spiritual in nature. He had avocados and mangoes and other various fruits, flower essences and rattles and drums and colorful hammocks and cushions all around. It was beautiful, and I was so touched. I was to be his first student. Miguel had spent 30 years in ashrams[2] in the Caribbean and much of his focus was as a yogi, but he was also writing a book of esoteric knowledge of his experiences on the Peruvian spiritual path.

It ended up that the "amenities" Miguel was referring to were electricity and running water. There weren't any. He did have a nice bathroom and a beautiful big bathtub, but there was no connection to water. He took me out of the compound to a small stream of ice cold water from the snowmelt of the surrounding mountains and told me that that was where he bathed every morning. In the bathroom, he had a huge plastic trash can filled with water and a bucket. At least there was a private, functioning toilet, though to flush it you had to scoop a bucket of water out of the trash can and dump it into the toilet.

It was very cold up there. Though the second story of the Temple was very beautiful, it was certainly not airtight, and he had stuffed rags in the openings where the windows and ceiling didn't quite meet with the walls. He had a stack of several thin, lumpy mattresses where I was meant to sleep. No matter how many different ways I rearranged those mattresses I never did find a way to avoid the lumps. Something else I hadn't considered was that there were only dirt roads up the mountain to his house.

---

[2] An ashram is a spiritual center of Hindu cultural activities such as yoga, meditation or religious instruction.

There were no road signs and many turns and forks.

I couldn't remember how to get up there even when I could find a taxi that was willing to try to take me. It was rainy season, and I had to be sure to get a taxi with a long enough chassis so that if it ended up in a mud pit, it could get out. Sometimes they were practically skating in the mud and it was downright scary. There was a bus that came up to the general area, but the Temple was across a huge field which was frequently flooded. So if I wanted to go into Cusco I had to make sure that I was back before dark, which was about 6:00 PM. And at 6:00 PM not only was it dark, but we also had no electricity, so I sat in the Temple in the cold and the dark by myself every evening, as Miguel retired early.

While I was still in Tampa packing my suitcases to come to Peru, something very strange had happened. I had treated myself to two huge healing stones—one was a two-foot high amethyst crystal cathedral which I kept in the living room and the other was a two-foot high, thick selenite sword which I kept in my bedroom. While I was packing my suitcases the selenite sword actually said to me, *Take me with you*. Well, needless to say, not only was I astounded to have another stone speak to me, it was big and heavy and impractical to take with me. It weighed eight pounds.

"But, but, but I thought we were roommates . . . ."

No, it said, *You are just the messenger. Take me to Miguel.*

I balked, "And besides, you are quite fragile and could break on the way."

Wrap me in a towel, and I will be fine. Take me to Miguel.

Bloody wonderful, now inanimate objects are speaking to me, bossing me around, telling me what to do.

Ferchrissake, that stone was not cheap! Oh, here we go again, just do as you're told, Lisa.

I always thought that rocks were just . . . well, rocks. There was even an expression that I used to use that I really liked: "He's got about as much personality as a box of rocks." Unless I was losing my mind, it was becoming apparent that rocks, indeed, did have character and preferences. Yeah, this revelation was actually going to change my life.

I wrapped the eight pound selenite sword in a purple towel and put it in my suitcase, as I had been instructed to do. When I got to the airport and they put the suitcase through the scanner the security guard said to me, "You have a rather large natural element here in your bag."

"Yes, yes, I know it's a big rock." I said rolling my eyes, not believing I was having this conversation.

The security guard said, "You are taking a ROCK to Peru!? I thought they had plenty of rocks there already . . . ." He shrugged his shoulders and passed my bag through.

****

Things didn't actually go so well with me staying at Miguel's Temple. Aside from the fact that it was cold and dark and isolated, things kept happening in Miguel's life that were taking him away from home, and he was really not around much to spend time with me. I felt abandoned. He had told me my meals would be provided, and one weekend he did have a cook, but for the most part we went into Cusco daily for a meal and I was left to my own devices most of the time. Miguel said that it was due to the selenite sword—that his life had gone crazy since I'd brought it. He meant that in a good way, but it really wasn't helping me much.

The little bit of time we did spend together, he had me meditate by myself while working with a collection of tiny glass bottles of holy water that he had collected from sacred sites around the world. I drank a few drops of the water to incorporate their energies within me. Twice he had me drink a pale green, gelatinous, and lumpy liquid at night before I went to bed (which I later learned was *wachuma*, a brew made from highland cacti) and then asked me how my dreams were the next morning. My father, who had passed 3 years before, did come to me in a dream, but other than that . . . nothing else memorable happened. Miguel kept getting called away, and I kept thinking I would go with him, but I was never invited. It was disappointing.

Once he left me alone up there for three days while he went to Lima to do an energetic clearing on the house of some politician. I was cold and scared and felt very vulnerable up there by myself, as there weren't even proper locks on the doors to my part of the Temple. I had to climb a vertical ladder to get to my area—the stairs were not yet fixed to the wall. This made middle-of-the-night trips to the toilet particularly tricky, as if the cold and dark weren't enough. So I turned something into a chamber pot to minimize the risk of crashing to my death in the night just because I needed to pee. Eventually, I decided to move back into Cusco into a hotel where I had access to the "amenities" to which I was accustomed.

There´s a Shaman in My Shower

One morning when I went for breakfast in the hotel, there was a group of maybe ten Americans chatting away in the breakfast room. I asked them where they were from and much to my surprise, they were from Tampa, Florida, my hometown. Now what were the chances of that happening?

They were a group of students from the University of South Florida and had two women who were a bit older accompanying them. One of the ladies looked to be in her 40s, and we struck up a conversation. The kids were going on a hike, and this lady wasn't particularly interested in going for a hike. She wanted to go shopping. I had been by myself up in the mountains for couple of weeks so I was happy to have some company, and I offered to take her shopping while the others went hiking.

We hung out in the breakfast room and chatted for a while, and I discovered that she was a teacher at the school that my son attended. She didn't know him personally because he wasn't in any of her classes, but I showed her a picture of him, and we talked about what a small world it was after all.

One day after Miguel had reappeared in Cusco, he stopped by the hotel to see me and while he was there I offered to let him use my bathroom to take a nice hot shower, since his only means of bathing was provided by the snowmelt stream in the field in front of his house. He gratefully accepted my offer.

I left the room to give him privacy and after a while I came back and saw that the small window to the bathroom was open and steam was billowing out. I could hear the water running so I knew he was still in the shower. I just waited in the hallway outside my room.

My new friend came by to meet me to go shopping at the agreed-upon time. She looked at me quizzically with the unspoken question while glancing up at the cloud of steam coming out of the bathroom window.

"Oh, I'm just waiting out here for a moment. There's a shaman in my shower . . . " Then we both cracked up laughing— the answer to the question really was just an opening for a number of other questions!

****

Jumping forward in time here: a couple of weeks later I was talking to my son in Tampa on the telephone when he said to me, "You'll never believe what happened today. One of my teachers was absent and so we had a substitute teacher. She was doing the roll call, and when she called my name she said, 'Jesse Sims, I saw your mother the other day.'

I said, 'No you didn't.' *Sassy kid. . . .*

'Yes, I did.'

'No you didn't.' *What a smart ass thing to say.*

'Yes, I did. She was in Cusco, Peru.'

"Well, Mom, my face just about slid off the front of my head. What are you doing spying on me from South America?"

Yes, yes, yes—it is a small world after all.

Kush

While I was still staying at the Temple, occasionally a friend of Miguel's, named Kush, would come and park his jeep inside the walled compound for safekeeping. Sometimes when Kush was going into town Miguel would ask him if we could catch a ride into Cusco with him rather than cross the fields and take the "combi" bus, also affectionately referred to as the "chicken bus," since there was also occasionally a live chicken or two on board. Sometimes after dark Kush would bring people to the downstairs of the Temple for what Miguel called "ceremony." I would be upstairs alone in the cold and dark, wondering what the hell I had gotten myself into, and I could hear them singing. Sometimes the smoke of incense or tobacco would waft up through the floorboards into my part of the Temple. Well, there was SO much going on that I didn't understand, and this was just one more thing.

I was staying in touch with a couple of the young girls I had met at the Spanish school and they told me that they were considering doing one of these "ceremonies" with Kush. They called it *Ayahuasca*. They said it was a form of spiritual healing using a brew made from a jungle vine which gave a sort of a visionary emotional and/or physical healing.

Okay, dancing around in the dark with rattles to Peruvian tribal music is one thing, but I really had no interest in drinking jungle juice. However, I was intrigued to learn more about something I'd never heard of, and it was surprising me that I kept hearing talk of this *Ayahuasca*.

Kush was about the same age as me, and he was a very quiet man. He only ever spoke directly to me if I spoke to him first. I found the combination of his self-assured manner and seemingly egoless, quiet personality quite intriguing. Plus he was doing healings with plant spirit medicines. I wanted to know more.

My girlfriends told me he had a shop in town and told me where it was located. When Miguel disappeared on me, I went to Kush's shop and asked him if he would work with me, teach me. I explained to him that I had come to Peru to study shamanism with Miguel, but Miguel had disappeared, and my time was limited in Peru—would he consider working with me?

The answer was no. I needed to wait for Miguel.

Other People's Shit

I decided to go with a group from the school on one of the excursions to the nearby town of Pisaq, to visit the market and ruins.

It was not one of the best days of my life.

We met up at the school and then walked over to the place where we were to catch the collectivo, which is a local van that you can take to get from one town to another in The Sacred Valley really cheaply. I can't say the place really qualified as a bus station; it was more of an opening in between the buildings with a dusty parking lot and a vehicle or two waiting to fill up while the driver stands in the road and shouts, "Pisaq! Pisaq! Pisaq!" I decided to use the bathroom before I got on the bus for the trip.

I've never seen a nastier bathroom.

The floor was wet with God-knows-what, and there was no place to hang my backpack, so I set it on top of the trash bin, forgetting that they never flush toilet paper in Peru. They throw it in the trash. The toilets don't flush—you have to pour a bucket of water in the toilet bowl to move anything. Well, the person in there prior to me had a serious case of the runs, and there was no bucket in sight. While I was squatting in mid-air, trying not to touch anything, I was focused on hitting the side of the bowl with my stream in an attempt to avoid splashing anything on me that was already in the toilet.

Well, much to my disgust, once we were en route to Pisaq, I realized that I had taken with me little clumps of somebody else's shit which had attached themselves to the bottom my backpack while it was sitting on top of the trash bin. So while I was crammed-packed into the sardine bus for an hour with my backpack on my lap for safe-keeping, I kept getting someone else's little clumps of shit on me. UGH!!

In the meantime, my eyes were running because the dust had blown in them, and my contact lenses were really irritating my eyes. I was also trying to prepare for a day in the sunshine by slathering myself with sunblock. In the end, my eyes were streaming tears from the sunblock, dust, and pollution, and I did not dare touch them in fear of going blind from God-knows-what bacteria on the OPS (Other People's Shit). You know that feeling you get when there is something in your eye and you just can't get it out? Well, I was pretty irritable by the time we got to Pisaq. Our guide led us to a clean bathroom with SOAP (no paper, but you can't have everything!!). I stayed there for about half an hour to recover and felt much better.

I knew it was a two-hour climb up to the ruins, so I was staying down in the town for an hour and a half, getting over the previous incident and perusing the market stalls. Then I took the 20-minute taxi ride up the mountain and met the group at the ruins. They were all 20-something and still, even after them climbing for two hours, I could not keep up with them. Most of the kids in the school were half my age and when they went on excursions they were more into "conquering the mountain" rather than meandering around, taking photos and smelling the flowers, as I was. After seeing the ruins, they decided to trek the two or three kilometers down the mountain.

I really thought climbing DOWN the mountain would be okay, but in the process I twisted my ankle, and I really had no choice but to go with them as we were miles away from any road where I might find an alternate way down. God only knows how I made it down that mountain. There was no real path. It was very steep with lots of rocks to stumble over. I was praying like there was no tomorrow, partly because I was scared half to death and partly to distract myself from the pain I was feeling in my ankle. They were much faster than I was going downhill, and so, periodically, they would wait for me to catch up. The moment I caught up they would take off again, so I never got a chance to catch my breath and reach equilibrium. By the time I got to the bottom, my ankle was black and swollen. Luckily a couple of the people on the excursion were medical students and helped me get what I needed for my ankle, but I was fairly crippled at that point.

We had arrived back in Cusco, and I was standing in the Main Plaza trying to catch a cab home. I was hopping around on one foot, and just using the other leg as a prop. My balance was precarious at best. A taxi had stopped for me and as I was loading my things into the cab while standing on one leg, the cab moved just a little bit and the open door bumped me. I found myself sitting on my ass in the middle of the road, traffic zipping by me left and right.

When I got back to the hotel, I went to my room, closed the door, and had a good cry.

The Dalai Lama Comes to Cusco

By this time, I had moved back into Cusco and was in a hotel in the San Blas district. Before Miguel's disappearance, he had gotten two tickets for us, which were in my possession, to a speech given by the Dalai Lama who was due to be in Cusco later that month.

The day came when the Dalai Lama was to make his appearance in Cusco, and Miguel was still not back. There was no way I could go alone with my ankle in the state it was in. My room was on the fourth floor of the hotel, which I liked because it had more light than the lower floors. But it also had no elevator, and getting down the stairs was incredibly painful, so I was just spending most of the time in my hotel room to give myself a chance to heal.

Kush had expressed a great interest in also going to see the Dalai Lama, but with Miguel's disappearance, he had been unable to get tickets. The Dalai Lama's appearance was set for 1:00 p.m., and at 10:00 a.m., with Miguel having been gone for ten days, I felt justified in calling Kush and offering him Miguel's ticket. But, I told him, there would be a catch: he would have to help me because I couldn't go alone with a sprained ankle. Would he like to join me?

We went together, and we sat together, and I was thinking that it took the Dalai Lama coming to town to finally make it possible for me to spend any time with Kush. We saw the Dalai Lama, and he spoke to us. It was tedious as they were translating from his very thickly accented English into Spanish and Quechua which took a lot of time and was difficult to follow. The whole time I was distracted by Kush's waist-length hair that was touching my arm. Some of the Q'ero elders (the indigenous descendants of the Inka) were there on the stage as well, and they had gifted the Dalai Lama with a coca leaf bag made from alpaca wool which he was wearing around his neck. Alpaca wool is some of the finest in the world, but the Dalai Lama was having a reaction to it, and he kept scratching the back of neck where the wool was touching it. The Dalai Lama strikes me as a practical man, in the end he had to remove it from around his neck. He spoke to the audience of about 400 for less than an hour. It was a very casual conversation, and though I'm sure just being in the same room with the Dalai Lama must have some kind of energetic influence, I didn't really receive any profound revelations.

In truth, I was kind of intimidated by Kush. I could barely speak, I was self-conscious of my bad Spanish. His gentle nature which was so very different to mine, I found fascinating, yet made me feel uncomfortable. However, I knew that I was in a pretty strong position to ask him one more time if he would work with me, so I gathered up my courage and asked him if he would do a personal healing for me.

He said yes. I was thrilled.

First, he wanted me to do a meditation with a group that he had that met weekly. Then, he asked me to come by his shop the next morning at 10:00 a.m., and he would do a reading. When I arrived, he pulled out what he called Oracle Cards with odd symbols on them. He laid the cards out on a table in front of me and he started.

"You have to do Ayahuasca," he told me.

"I can't do Ayahuasca. I'm on medication to help me with my anxiety," I told him. I'd done a bit of investigation on Ayahuasca as it kept coming up, and I kept hearing about it. I was somewhat relieved to know that the medication I was on would prevent me from being able to have to participate in one of these ceremonies.

"That's no problem," he said, "A good shaman can drink it for you. I will drink the medicine, and you will receive the healing."

Well, I certainly wasn't expecting that!

"Okay," I said hesitantly, a bit stunned. We set a date and time.

I walked back to the hotel, shaking my head the whole way, trying to get this to sink in and a bit dumbstruck at what I had just agreed to do.

Ayahuasca

The Ayahuasca ceremony took place in the downstairs section of Miguel's Temple—so I was back where I had started. There were cushions and blankets and empty buckets scattered around. Besides myself and Kush, there was one other couple. Kush had set up an altar that had all kinds of intriguing items on it— crystals, stones, jungle rattles and other rattles made from the leaves of plants, incense burners, various incenses, gigantic tobacco cigarettes, condor feathers, drums, and a plastic bottle filled with a dark brown liquid. In his usual manner and without explanation, Kush came in, put a ceremonial robe on over his clothes, sat down quietly, lit a candle and one of the gigantic tobacco cigarettes, inhaled deeply, closed his eyes, and blew tobacco smoke over the various items on the altar. He lined up some small ceramic cups and poured the brown liquid from the plastic bottle into them. He blew tobacco smoke over the cups and whispered an unusual-sounding prayer that I couldn't understand over each cup with a distinctive blowing of air through his teeth which didn't quite qualify as a whistle. He handed a cup to each of the other participants and took one for himself, suggesting that they drink it quickly as the taste was pretty bad. Then he chuckled to himself and knocked his cup back in one gulp. He shook his head quickly making the sound that one makes when they've just swallowed something with a very strong taste. He breathed out a "Whaaaaaa . . ." and waited for the others to follow suit. Apparently the taste was foul, as they both grimaced and also shook their heads, then took a deep breath, now resigned to fate. Kush then asked if there were any questions.

The couple, Ian from England and Giselle from France, asked various questions like how long before it took effect, how long would it last and where the bathrooms were. I just sat and listened, feeling quite relieved that I didn't have to drink the brew and very interested to see what would happen. After about

40 minutes, Kush got up and went to the bathroom and threw up. He then came back into the maloca and blew out the flame of the single candle that had been illuminating the room as night had fallen since we started the ceremony. Shortly thereafter Ian staggered to his feet saying, "I'm gonna hurl!" and bolted out the door of the Temple for the bathroom. A couple of minutes later he returned saying, "Maybe not." This happened several times with Ian, and every time he struggled to get the door open, bolting out without closing it properly which allowed a blast of cold air to rush in, and returning a couple minutes later saying, "Maybe not." It actually got to be quite comical to watch. Giselle had begun a quiet crying and whimpering, and after a while she vomited into one of the buckets.

After another half hour or so the two became very quiet, apparently going inside themselves on this visionary healing journey. Giselle quietly cried for quite a long time while Ian mumbled to himself something I couldn't understand. Kush went over to each of them, whispering questions like, "Are you all right?" and doing other things which I couldn't make out because of the darkness.

After he had tended to them both, he came over to me. I was sitting up cross-legged on a cushion on the floor, and he told me to lie down. In our initial discussions about specifically what it was I wanted to heal, I had told Kush that I had had an ongoing problem with my thyroid gland for the past 15 years. I had refused to take medication for it because I'd been told that once I started the medication I would have to take it for the rest of my life, and I really didn't like the idea of being dependent on medications. My thyroid had begun to grow nodules and had become a multi-nodular goiter, though it wasn't evident by my appearance. That was one thing I wanted to heal, and the other thing I wanted to heal was my broken heart. It had been three years since I'd left my husband and though I had been the one that had initiated our separation, he'd seemed to have recovered pretty quickly. I was still very attached to my disappointment that the lifelong commitment we had made had disintegrated.

It had been more than three years since I'd been touched by a man. Though I felt that I may never again have what it takes to have another relationship, I was desperately lonely and craving the touch of a man.

Kush came over to me and told me to lie back on the cushions, and I did. He then leaned over me and, without any explanation, put his mouth on my neck and began to suck. I had an instant orgasm, three years of pent-up energy which left my body convulsing. Kush then leaned over and vomited into one of the buckets. I laid there with my body trembling for the next half hour, having no idea whatsoever had just happened. After a while Kush came over and said to me, "They were snakes, and they didn't want to leave." I had no idea or interest at this stage of what Ian and Giselle were doing because what I had just experienced was so intense that I was just reeling from it. It might qualify as one of the most humbling, profound, and humiliating experiences of my life.

I lost track of time as I lay there in the dark, and after the waves of my experience had subsided Kush came back over and sat beside me. He asked me to tell him about my family. He asked if he could see a picture of my family, and I had one in my wallet which I showed to him. He asked me to say their names, and then he asked me about my ancestry. Well, that was quite a topic for discussion.

I told Kush the stories that I had been told about my ancestry. Three of my grandparents had already passed on before I was born so I only ever knew my father's father. I told him about my parents, and I told him what I knew of my parent's parents. He took particular interest in the story of my father's side of the family.

My father was born in 1922 in Nashville, Tennessee. Three years later, his twin sisters were born. My father's parents lived with his mother's parents, and apparently that was a difficult situation. My grandfather wanted to move out of her house, but my grandmother refused to, so when my father was three years old his father left them.

When my father was five, his mother died. I was told that the death certificate listed tuberculosis as the cause of death, but my father was always suspicious as to whether that was true. He told me that he was with her when she died, that she had asked him to go to the store and buy her a box of vanilla wafer cookies. He said he brought them back to her, and she was lying in bed sick, but that she went to take a bite of a vanilla wafer, and died with the vanilla wafer still between her teeth.

So my father and his twin sisters were raised by their grandparents. According to my father's account, my great-grandmother was mentally ill. He told us stories of the abuse that he suffered at her hands. He said he never knew why it was he was being beaten with electrical cords or stomped on with high heeled shoes—it never made any sense to him.

When he was 11 years old, his grandfather died. He always suspected that his grandmother had poisoned him with arsenic, and he remembered his grandfather throwing up green matter in the sink at the time before he died. Although they were very poor, I always got the impression that they came from a higher social class. My great uncles who were raised as older brothers to my father were quite well-educated and successful. My father used to tell us that as a child he was so poor that he would hide at lunch time in school so no one would notice that he didn't have any lunch. He would jump the trains and ride the boxcars to get to school. I always felt lucky as a child that I never had to suffer like my father and mother did growing up during The Depression Era in the southern United States.

When my father was 13 years old, one night his grandmother was found in her nightgown digging up her husband's grave in the snow. At that point, she was put in a mental institution. The children's father was found living in Alabama, and they were shipped off to live with him. Over the next few years my great-grandmother attempted and failed to commit suicide six times, each time by slitting her wrists. The seventh time she was finally successful when she slit her own throat.

My father was named after his father and when his father left, his grandparents renamed him. They used his middle name and their last name and his father was always referred to as "That Devil." So you can imagine that things didn't go so smoothly when the children who had suffered so much loss in their young years were shipped off to live with someone who they believed to be the devil.

My grandfather was a traveling horse harness salesman who had just inherited three children who had been raised to hate him. His work required that he travel, and he would have to leave the children alone for days at a time. I was told that my grandfather had tried to stay in contact with them after he left my grandmother, when they were young, but that he had been denied access. He didn't even know these children, and he had no experience or parenting skills, and so he beat them. My father said that when he was 15 years old and they were living in Alabama in the late 1930s, his father was beating him with a piece of horse harness. A black man who worked for my grandfather stepped in and said, "I'm sorry, Sir, but if you hit that boy again, I'm going to have to stop you." My father told that story as if not only had that black man saved his life, but that he had risked his own life by speaking out the way he did in that time and that place.

When he was 15, my father got permission to move out of his father's house, and he moved into a boarding house where he finished out high school, became the president of his senior class, and the editor of the school newspaper. A couple of years later, he joined the U.S. Army Air Corps and became a pilot flying troop carriers during World War II. He met my mother in Florence, South Carolina, and they corresponded during the war. My mother kept all his letters to her, which were shared with us as children (if we were interested), though she destroyed hers to him. They were married in 1944 when my mother was 18 years old and my father was 21.

When I told Kush this story, it was with an attitude of "Oh, let me tell you about my crazy family." In truth, I had always feared my great grandmother's mental illness because we never knew what it really was, and I feared that it might be hereditary. (I had a wonderful medical intuitive homeopath in England who suspected that it was syphilis—there was no cure for it at the time). So my attitude was one of bravado masking the fear that I had of coming from a crazy family. Though my father never showed any signs whatsoever of mental illness, his twin sisters who were three years younger than him had probably been much more affected by the events of their young lives than he had been, and they both had very challenging personalities.

Kush listened to my story, and when I was finished, he went away for a while. In between the times when he was speaking to us, he would play his drum or shake his rattle and sing his ceremonial Ayahuasca songs, which I later learned were called *Icaros*. After he had communed with his guiding spirits (which is apparently what he was doing when he was singing), he came back over and squatted down beside me and said, "There is a problem. You need to do a ceremony to honor the spirits of your ancestors. You have been holding them in an energy which is not helpful for you or for them. You must do a ceremony and call in their spirits to honor and forgive them and also to forgive yourself." He also told me, "You are not ready to heal your broken heart yet. You need more time."

It had probably been four or five hours since they'd drunk the Ayahuasca and the energy had shifted significantly. Kush was now very loquacious and sitting at the altar in the dark, telling us stories about how humanity needed to change its "cosmic chip". Every time he would say this he would crack up laughing, and I can't count how many times he said "cosmic chip". It really was funny, actually quite surreal and good-natured. He was saying, "I don't know why I'm talking so much, I don't usually talk this much. I bet you're all thinking, 'I wish this guy would shut up!'" And then he would crack up laughing again. A little while later everybody started dozing off, and Kush offered to take us back down to our places in Cusco for the rest of the night.

****

31

When I woke up the next morning, I could not stop crying. I felt so incredibly humbled by the sincerity of the ceremony the night before and by Kush's words, which I felt in my heart were true. I felt like a fool. How could I be so stupid?! How could I pass judgment over people whom I've never met, my own ancestors? I did the ceremony that day. I lit candles in my hotel room and I called in their spirits and I asked their forgiveness and I cried most of the afternoon. So much pain and so much fear. I released it all that day.

****

It was a very profoundly healing experience for me, and I became intrigued by the power of the Ayahuasca ceremony. I felt that a door had been opened for me. I felt humbled and privileged to have had that experience, and the next day I went by Kush's shop and expressed my deepest gratitude to him for sharing this amazing experience with me. With humble sincerity, I asked him if he would teach me more. I had decided that if the experience was that profound for me just being present in an Ayahuasca ceremony, what would it be like if I had drunk it myself? So I decided to stop taking my medication, and my research told me that there was a two week half-life to get the drugs out of my system. After two weeks, I went back and asked Kush if I could do another ceremony but this time drink the Ayahuasca myself, which he agreed to do.

Kush and his fiancé, Erica, had been building a house of their own near Miguel's Temple and in those two weeks he had completed a small structure on his own property. I had asked Kush if I could do the ceremony alone, which is not typical. I felt so self-conscious that I was concerned that it would have an effect on my experience if other people were present, and he agreed to do it with me alone. It was to be the first ceremony in what was to become Kush's own ceremonial healing center and home. It was freshly painted that day and before we started the ceremony he blessed and initiated the building by saying prayers and spraying Ayahuasca from his mouth in every corner of the room.

I had done quite a bit of research on Ayahuasca before I drank it myself. I had learned that it requires a special diet prior to imbibing it and that the experience itself was frequently viewed as a form of death and could be quite frightening, even terrifying. The fear itself of the experience could be a huge obstacle to one's personal experience in healing. I truly felt at that point that I had been through so much emotional pain that if I died during this experience, that was a viable option.

The second ceremony was absolutely nothing like the first. I drank the Ayahuasca and laid down on the mat. Within 30 minutes I was launched into another dimension which defies description. It took every fiber of my being and consciousness to be present in this place. It felt as if all of the molecules of my being would fly off in 1,000 different directions, and I would just dissolve if I did not hold my consciousness together. I was physically paralyzed, I could not move or speak. It was quite a cold night in May, which is just coming up on Peruvian winter and it is not customary there to use indoor heating. I later saw there were ice crystals outside on the windows.

This ceremony was not healing for me in the way that the first ceremony was. But it certainly changed me in many ways. For one, I know for a fact that other dimensions exist because I was there. I saw colors I have never seen before or since. It was nothing like anything I'd read of anyone else's descriptions of the places they had been during Ayahuasca's journeys—which are frequently tropical or celestial worlds. It was a metallic world, and very cold. It was so cold that I couldn't stop shivering. I daresay my body was quaking, and Kush kept piling blankets on top of me until I thought the weight of them would crush me. I was so, so cold. I just wanted to touch something warm. I wished Kush would touch me, but he didn't. Earlier in the day I'd been petting a cat, and now, I longed for that cat to sit in my lap just to touch something warm. The general sentiment I was having at that time in my life was that people in my life were so demanding, and I just wanted to be left alone. And I felt that Ayahuasca was saying to me, "You want to be alone? This is what it feels like to be alone. You are a human being, you are a social being, you are not an island, and this is what it feels like to be alone." It was not a pleasant experience.

The logical part of my mind could hear Kush singing in the background. He was dancing and making music and all I could think was, "How can he possibly be singing and moving while under the effects of Ayahuasca when I am completely paralyzed?"

That experience was quite a shock to my physical being and my belief system. I wanted to know more. I asked Kush if I could assist him in future ceremonies, and he agreed to allow me to do that. After getting off my meds, over the next couple of weeks I sat in on four more ceremonies. Most of Kush's clients are non-native people, and the most popular language spoken is English. Kush does speak English, but with my help, he was able to go much deeper in conversation with the people he was working with. From my standpoint, I had become intrigued that a person is able to function consciously while under the influence of Ayahuasca. The next session I only took a half dose, and I found that I was not able to remain consciously in the room. My mind kept going off into other experiences, so I found that if I took only a quarter dose that I could remain conscious and helpful. I got to where I could begin to recognize some of the different energies that Kush was calling in during the ceremonies. It was truly fascinating.

Back to the USA

It appeared that my plan to move to Peru with the children was really not feasible. The school systems would not meld together well, and I decided that though my son would love Peru, my daughter would hate it. She can be a bit of a princess when it comes to certain things, and the under-developed-ness of Peru would not appeal to her at all. Well, that was okay, I could wait another 4 or 5 years until my children were launched, and then I would move back to Peru. So I buckled down. I managed to find an administrative job that paid well, working for a real estate agent, and just got on with the business of raising my children and paying my bills.

I had my thyroid gland checked, and much to my disappointment, I found that it was continuing to grow, and it was becoming a bit uncomfortable. I had really been quite convinced that the healing that I had received in Peru had had a positive effect, but that stepping back into my old life and all of its demands and responsibilities and the energies that I had been finding so challenging in the past had reactivated the problem. I had medical insurance through my husband's work, and at the recommendation of my endocrinologist, I decided to go ahead and have surgery.

The surgeon removed my entire thyroid—there were hundreds of nodules all over it which they were concerned could become cancerous. I won't say I was happy about it, and I wasn't happy to know that I would have to be on thyroid medication for the rest of my life which I had spent the past 15 years trying to avoid in every way shape and form. I had even learned that my MD was also an intuitive medical doctor. I asked him what this was with my thyroid.

He said, "It is *fear*."

No joke! Of course it is *fear*, it is always fear in some form or another.

"I don't know, Lisa. It's like the information is being blocked. All I am getting is "*fear*."

So I went ahead and had the surgery. At least it was over and done with and I didn't have to think about it anymore. I was working on getting my physical body healthy again. Due to years of long-term stress, many of the neurotransmitters in my body were at dangerously low or nonexistent levels. I was using TAAT (targeted amino acid therapy) to raise the levels of serotonin, dopamine, adrenalin, and epinephrine in my body. It took a couple of years, but things were definitely improving.

I had a wonderful group of loving, supportive friends that I had met through the metaphysical spiritual center. There were various circles of people that I met with two or three times a week—study groups of various kinds and a lot of opportunities to socialize. On Sunday afternoons, we would frequently go to lunch together and occasionally meet at the house of one of my friends to watch a movie.

One Sunday, the movie happened to be about Peruvian Shamanism. I had just had the thyroid surgery the week before and still had bandages on my neck. After the movie was over, my friend asked me if I would share my experiences with Ayahuasca with the group since no one else present had ever done it before.

So I launched off into my story about my first Ayahuasca experience. When I got to the part where my great-grandmother had finally succeeded in killing herself by cutting her own throat, I dramatized it with a sweeping motion of my finger across my neck. I paused for effect and glanced at my friends who were staring at me with looks of amazement on their faces.

"What did you just say, Lisa?!"

I started to repeat myself, and then I got it. I froze mid-sentence. There I was with a four-inch wound across my neck. These were dear friends of mine, and they knew about my struggles with trying to heal my thyroid and the challenges I had faced in looking for the cause of this condition in my body.

It was so obvious! Why didn't I see this before? Why had I struggled for years resisting medication and treatment while looking for a cause and a noninvasive solution to treating this?

Why had my medical intuitive not been given access to something that was so blatantly obvious?

I went home and called my sister and told her about it, and we both cried. Kush was right, this condition was related to the fear that I had felt of my ancestry and my great-grandmother's mental illness and suicide. It had manifested itself physically in me through this multi-nodular goiter in the same location on my body where she had eventually succeeded in taking her own life. This was an ancestral wound. And for reasons I have never understood, I had to surrender to the surgery before the answer was revealed to me as to its origin.

Another Trip to Peru –
Are You Kidding Me??

It was late afternoon when I received the phone call that no mother ever wants to receive. It was November 2008, and the woman said to me, "You had better come quickly. I am with your son and he needs to go the hospital." Every fiber of my being went on alert. "He has been badly beaten and he's not making a lot of sense." She put Jesse on the telephone and he was breathless and panicked, but at least he was talking so that was a good sign. She got back on the phone and told me where they were located.

I have never moved so fast in my life. In five seconds, I was in my car driving to where he was which was about three miles away. I called in the Reiki energies[3] as I drove, holding the steering wheel with the heels of my hands. The energies poured through me until my hands were practically on fire, pointing in the direction of where I knew he was. I was feeling very grateful in that moment to have the Reiki to give me something positive to work with and focus on until I could get there.

Jesse had not been doing too well. He was 16 years old and hanging around with the wrong people. He was failing in school, and although in the past he had been placed in the "gifted" programs, he had been kicked out of all of those due to poor performance and absence. He was getting into all sorts of trouble, refusing to let us know where he was, and it was getting pretty scary.

When my husband and I separated, we sold the big house that we owned together and bought two smaller houses that were within walking distance of each other so that the children had easy access to us both. We made sure to stay in the same school

---

[3] Reiki is an energetic healing modality from Japan in which I had received initiations and was using in my spiritual practice.

district so that our children had the same friends and teachers, in hopes of minimizing the impact of the trauma of our separation.

Jesse insisted on living with his father, saying that he didn't want to leave him alone. Our family therapist thought that the real reason he wanted to stay with his father was that his father was not really paying much attention to him—he was so engrossed in his own life that it was really more like my son was living alone and got to do whatever he wanted. Unfortunately, his choices were not the best.

I had sought advice regarding the situation to see what I could possibly do to influence things. I had learned that once a child reaches the age of 14, if one were to go to court, the judge is going to ask the child what he wants to do. Unless there is a concrete reason to rule otherwise, the judge is going to favor in the direction of the child's preferences, so I didn't really see any point in pursuing that avenue. I mean, who am I to come between Jesse and his father? I figured they had their own karma[4] between them.

It is so strange to me that the more you love someone the greater the fear is of losing that person. I had always had a nagging fear that one day I would lose one of my children, a horrible feeling. I had actually promised myself that if and when that day came, rather than allowing it to ruin the rest of my life, I would instead be grateful for every blessed day that I had had them in my life.

And it has happened. In particular, I felt I had lost Jesse on more than one occasion, though thankfully, it has never happened physically. I'd lose him sometimes for months at a time. He is not good at staying in touch with me, and then when he does, the communication that I do get is cryptic and sometimes unsettling.

And this was one of those times that I truly felt I had lost him. I felt so helpless, watching him make poor choices and having so little control over being able to influence them. How

---

[4] Karma is a key concept in Hinduism and Buddhism of the principle of causality, where intent and actions of an individual influence the future in their soul's path and its interactions with others.

could it be that you could love someone and feel so much pain as a result of that love?? It was brutal.

Time stood still as I was driving to find my son. It seemed an eternity and yet it was only minutes. My son had been with one of his friends in a movie theater when his friend, who was a very large and strong young man, had said something to provoke another young man that they went to school with. The young man had called several of his friends, and after Jesse and his friend left the movie theater and were in the parking lot, they were jumped by this gang of boys. Of course, they didn't choose the big guy to beat up but Jesse, who was considerably smaller. Once he was down on the ground, they kicked and beat him mercilessly, until some kind person ran over to stop them. His head was covered in huge lumps from the kicking he'd received.

I drove to the emergency room and had him checked out. Luckily, with the exception of a minor concussion, he was going to be okay. I found it very interesting that although this happened outside of school hours and off the school grounds the administration of his school took it upon themselves to become involved. Of course, the relationship between these boys was a result of the fact that they went to school together. The administration was very good, and they were aware of the problematic relationships and situations that these boys were in, and I was grateful for that. At this stage in my life, I needed all the help I could get with the difficulties we found ourselves in. Even then it felt like the help that was available to me still wasn't enough. I'm a pretty resourceful person, but the situations in which I was finding myself, I had absolutely no clue how to handle at times.

I had started a new job within the previous six months, but the economy was not working in our favor. As a result, the company was having to downscale dramatically, and since I was their most recent hire, I was in the process of losing my job.

Back to my meditation practice, here we go again . . .

"Yes, I do know that these things happen for a reason, but it is absolutely beyond me what the hell is going on. I know this is an opening to what is going to happen next, but would you guys be so kind as to fill me in on what to do here? Jesse is in a crisis, I am losing my job . . . . Somebody please tell me what to do next."

Take Jesse to Peru. The message was in my head, but it was very clear.

"Oh, ferchrissake! You must be kidding me, not Peru again!?! How in the world am I going to do that?? It is November, it is the middle of the school year, and I thought we were done with Peru!!!"

Take Jesse to Peru. Just do it.

"Honestly! Okay, FINE!"

I thought, "How in the world am I going to swing this one!? I don't know…. But I have learned this much: sometimes I just have to show up and see what happens."

I made an appointment with the school principal. I walked into her office and sat down in the chair in front of her desk. I had no idea what I was going to say. I opened my mouth, and these words came out: "I'm thinking of taking my son to Peru."

I was absolutely flabbergasted when I heard her say, "What a good idea!"

Are you kidding me!?!? That was really not the response I was expecting, and I felt renewed hope.

She said, "Okay, let's see how we can do this. If you can wait till the end of this quarter, which is in about three weeks, that would be good timing. We'll look at it as if you are withdrawing him from school and moving to Peru. Then, let's just say that it becomes apparent that living in Peru is not going to work out, so you move back here and re-enroll him in school. What I could do then would be this: because he will be lacking third quarter grades, whatever grades he gets for the fourth quarter, I will just double. We'll do what we need to do to get that process started."

I was astonished, and I walked out of her office and down the hallway shaking my head and marveling at the course things were taking here. Boy, was I grateful for the power of the guidance of my unseen spiritual helpers! Since I started listening to them my life had unfolded in ways I could have never imagined or made happen on my own. I could always tell when they were at work—when whatever was happening was never something I could have come up with by myself.

Jesse was thrilled when I told him about the plan to go to Peru. I felt grateful and hopeful for the first time in a long time. Maybe I would have a chance to get my beautiful lost boy back.

I booked a flight leaving on Christmas Day. For one thing, most people don't want to travel on Christmas Day so most of the other flights were either already booked or outrageously expensive. Secondly, I really didn't like Christmas Day anymore. Since our family had split up it had become more complicated and a prime day to bring up all kinds of unresolved emotions and I usually ended up in tears. My daughter was in a relationship and was preferring to spend her time with her boyfriend's family. Understandably so—our little family was so fragmented and dysfunctional. Having the four of us all in one room at the same time was tortuous for me; the emotions ran so high. Christmas had just become so emotionally charged for me that I practically felt like I was suffering from PTSD from it, so I was just as happy to skip it altogether.

An interesting thing happened while organizing this trip. Of course, I had been to Peru twice before and all my friends knew that I was absolutely smitten with it. I invited my dear friend, Roger, to join us. He had been the one to help me through my thyroid surgery and recovery. He had been to South America and had worked with Ayahuasca. He was also on the Andean spiritual path.

I had met Roger just after the return from my second trip to Peru in 2006, and our friendship had really taken off. There was nothing that I had done that was too weird for him or that he hadn't done himself. He brought out a very playful side of me which I desperately needed. Of course, I hadn't had a close relationship with a man since I had left my husband. I felt very safe with Roger. He had been on a monastic path and had very nearly joined a monastery. He was very down-to-earth, having grown up as a farm boy, and though he had a degree in

Architecture, he had decided that he didn't like the culture around that occupation, and instead chose to work in carpentry and truck driving. He became a "true blue" and trusted friend.

After a few months of friendship with Roger, I asked him if he would help me. I was so missing the physical closeness of having a relationship with a man. I asked Roger if he would just lie with me in bed and hold me—it had been so long! As we laid there for a very long time with his arms wrapped around me, it felt as if puzzle pieces were coming back together within me. Whenever he came to my house to visit me he would walk through the front door and into the foyer and he would wrap his arms around me in a bear hug and just hold me. He was never the first to let go. Eventually I would just relax and breathe into it. It was the first step in healing my broken heart–that much I knew. I renamed him RogerBear. We developed a ritual where *instead* of dinner, we would go into the kitchen and devour concoctions we created with *Unconditional Chocolate* ice cream, strawberries and bananas–all slathered in chocolate syrup, nuts and whipped cream. Absolute Heaven!

I was looking for a little moral support in this upcoming venture, and I trusted Roger. He had been a wonderful friend for years and was someone I turned to when I needed clarity, perspective or emotional support. I would call him on the phone and pour my heart out to him about whatever was causing turmoil in my life. I remember one time I was feeling so emotional in the midst of my story that I had lost the ability to speak—my throat had such a huge lump in it. I was quiet for a few moments when Roger said, "Ah, this is the silence before the tears." He was my soft place to land. Our friendship was worth its weight in gold!

My plan when we arrived in Peru was to put my son in Spanish school and a volunteering program to work with orphans in hope of giving him another perspective on life. This would also get him away from the negative influences—hopefully, I could then have some influence on the future direction of his life.

When my friends heard that I was going to Peru, I started getting phone calls asking if they could come with us. They had never been to Peru, most didn't speak Spanish, and they knew that I had experience in Peru, and so they wanted to join me. Next thing I knew, there were six of us going, and I found myself in the position of being a tour conductor for my first small group.

On Christmas Day of 2008, the six of us flew to Cusco. On my second trip to Peru, I had made the acquaintance of a South African woman who owned the hostel where one of my friends had been staying. It was a fun and funky little place up in the San Blas district. I contacted her and made arrangements for us to stay there. The three extra people would stay there for three weeks, and then Roger, my son and I would stay for ten weeks.

The first two weeks I enrolled Jesse in the Spanish school and placed him in a homestay with a local family which was arranged by the school. This was the same school that I had attended two and a half years before. Jesse didn't speak any Spanish. I thought this was a good start and would put him on a different track. It also freed me up to spend some time showing my friends around my favorite places in Cusco and the Sacred Valley.

This first group was quite a learning experience for me. Two members of our group became very sick. One was due to a combination of altitude sickness, digestive issues, and sinus/breathing problems. This was exacerbated by him becoming badly burned by the sun, which is stronger at high altitudes (Cusco has some of the strongest UV rays in the world). He spent most of his time in bed, and as soon as he was healthy enough, he just flew back home. The other sick person had had pneumonia a couple of times previously, and her lungs were weak. As a result, the oxygen level in her blood was down to 65%, which was dangerously low. She was ordered to stay in bed at the hostel with an oxygen tank. She was loaded up to the eyeballs with so many drugs that when I went in her room, she was propped up in bed on stacks of pillows with a beautiful smile on her face. She was saying, "I don't even need to go to any of these places with you; I'm having a mystical experience right here in my room. Just look! The whole room is filled with angels!"

I thought, "Oh, my God, please don't die. I don't have any idea how to ship a body back to the United States!"

Wachuma

There is a cactus that grows in the high Andes which has been used by the native people for thousands of years in a ceremonial and healing way. In Quechua, this cactus is known as *Wachuma*. It is used in a similar way that the North American Native Americans use peyote.

Wachuma is not just a cactus. In the Andean tradition, everything has a spirit. When you take the body of the cactus into your own body, you are also taking in the spirit of Wachuma.

The cactus is prepared by removing the spines and the skin and boiling down parts of the body of the cactus. This creates a greenish brown, gelatinous liquid which is then consumed by the people involved in the ceremony. One of the active ingredients in this brew is the hallucinogen mescaline— as is also found in peyote.

During my third trip to Peru, the hostel where our little group was staying in San Blas was La Casa de la Gringa, and the owner, Lesley Myburgh, is a Wachumera—a shaman who specializes in working with this plant spirit medicine for healing purposes. Casa de la Gringa has become a bit of a temple for people who come from all around the world to work with Wachuma.

When the Spanish arrived to Peru in the 1500s, they also became familiar with this medicine. Taking Wachuma into your body creates an altered state of consciousness and sometimes hallucinatory effects. The Spanish were so awestruck by the effects that they likened it to heaven, and they renamed the cactus San Pedro (St. Peter), the holder of the keys to the gates of heaven.

The words Wachuma and San Pedro are used interchangeably in Cusco. In most parts of the world, the use of these plant spirit medicines has been made illegal because of the hallucinatory properties in both Wachuma and Ayahuasca.

It is my opinion that when used with reverence, proper guidance, and understanding, these plant spirit medicines can make it possible to open the doors to other realms. It is possible to gain insight into ourselves and the world in which we live. Plant spirit medicines can potentially heal emotional and physical issues.

Working with these plants is legal in Peru and some other South American countries. It has been documented that they have been used there for thousands of years. Many of the people who use them are working towards becoming more enlightened. It has been written that one ceremony of working with these plant medicines can be equivalent to the understanding gained by 10 years of meditation or therapy. People come from all over the world to work with these plants in Peru. It has become known as Esoteric Tourism.

There is a section at the back of this book with more information and resources about working with these plants. These are very powerful experiences, and one should never take working with these medicines lightly. I highly recommend that lots of research and inner work be done before considering taking any of these medicines. If they are not done in the right environment and with proper reverence, it is possible to do more damage than good. When you are working with these plant spirit medicines, you are energetically very open and vulnerable.

****

I had been hearing about San Pedro ever since my second trip to Peru. It wasn't really speaking to me at the time. I was going through my own powerful healing processes with Ayahuasca, which was just about all I could handle. San Pedro has a reputation for being a much gentler healing spirit than Ayahuasca. I had done a lot of healing work over the past couple of years, and I knew that I still had a way to go. Some of us in our little group decided to do a San Pedro ceremony with Lesley while we were there.

Lesley has a gorgeous home and magnificent gardens up on the mountain near The Temple of the Moon right smack in between Miguel's house and Kush's house.

We joined with some others in Lesley's garden early one morning. The garden was virtually exploding with flowers, hummingbirds, and hundreds of San Pedro cacti. We formed a circle, said our prayers, and stated our intentions. We then each drank a glass of the brew which had a slimy texture similar to that of aloe (and was not nearly as bad tasting as Ayahuasca, thank God!). The goal was to drink the whole glassful in one go without gagging.

I laid on a mat on the ground under a willow tree, and I saw the world anew. Where Ayahuasca took me inside of myself and other dimensions, one of San Pedro's gifts is a feeling of connection to everything outside of yourself. There is a feeling of oneness with the flowers and birds and the clouds. I could sense Mother Earth breathing. I felt infinitesimally small and simultaneously one with everything, a beautiful paradox.

I spent the morning in the garden lying on my mat, watching the clouds and feeling at one with the universe. I didn't really have much of a choice since getting up off the mat would have been an insurmountable feat. I was fairly immobilized.

The light! I was able to see light in ways that I had never seen light before. It is hard to describe; it was not that things were just brighter; it was that I could see *the light* in everything! The light was a form of consciousness that had its own being!

A hummingbird landed nearby me. It noticed me, cocked its head to one side the way birds do, and it looked at me intently. I *felt* it think *Oh, look! That human is awake!* And then I knew that it knew that I knew that it knew that I was *awake*. It was a defining moment for me—a transcendent moment in time.

I closed my eyes and the back of my eyelids became an Etch-A-Sketch. Little castles began drawing themselves in a beautiful terra-cotta shade of orange. When I opened my eyes, they disappeared. Then I closed my eyes, and they drew themselves again on the inside of my eyelids, each time a slightly different design, but mostly in the style of St. Basil's Cathedral in Russia, with its onion-shaped domes.

With my eyes closed, there were colors in the inner and outer corners of my eyes that I had never seen before, mostly turquoises and purples. I felt I could swim in those colors—they were so beautiful.

There was a small willow tree draped over the area where I was lying. It struck me as so sensuous, like it was dancing in the breeze. There were spider webs draped like little hammocks up in the trees above me, and they caught the light and looked at times as if they were on fire.

I had no concept whatsoever of time. Lesley would stop by occasionally and ask me how I was doing or if I needed anything. My answer to everything was "I don't know."

By the afternoon, I was able to walk around. Roger and I decided to go for a walk outside of the garden to the area around the Temple of the Moon. There are many open fields and huge rock outcroppings. Some of the stones had been carved by some ancient people in the shape of a condor head or hollowed out to make the shape of a llama. The Inka Trail passes between Lesley's garden and The Temple of the Moon. It is a very powerful place, full of magical energy.

There were some dogs running up and down the rock outcroppings, playing and barking. One in particular had what appeared to be some kind of animal pelt in her mouth. She and another dog were running up and down the mountain. They were having so much fun just being dogs.

Back behind us was a stone wall which surrounded a pasture. Inside the pasture was an alpaca and her pure white baby. The dog with the animal pelt in her mouth came tearing down the mountain past us and ran into the pasture with the alpacas. She started running in circles around them and barking.

Roger and I watched this with what started out to be amusement. Within a short time, it became apparent that the alpacas were frightened, and they began to call out for help.

I said to Roger that maybe he had better run over there and see if he could break it up, and I would run back to the house and get some help. Just then three other dogs joined the one in the field that was harassing the alpacas. I had been in this area long enough to know that there were three or four dogs that lived there. I was assuming that those dogs had gone over there to help protect their alpaca, since that was where they lived.

I ran back to the house and asked for someone to go help, and I just went back in the house. All that activity and excitement was a bit overwhelming in my altered state. I was standing in the kitchen a short while later when Roger walked in. I asked him how it went, and then I noticed that there were tears running down his cheeks.

He said, "It was too late. They killed the baby."

"What?!?" I said, "Are you sure?"

"Yes, Lisa, it died in my arms. I felt it take its last breath. When the other dogs ran over, they separated the baby from its mother and killed it. Once the dogs were gone I laid his little body down there with his mother, as you can imagine she was extremely upset. By then, the people who owned the land and alpacas were on their way over from the fields. So sad."

Wow! We just cried. Even under normal circumstances that would've been quite an experience, but in our altered states, we were completely blown away.

A couple of days later we were back at Casa de la Gringa having coca leaf readings by a renowned shaman known as Amado. Roger went first. The incident with the alpacas and the San Pedro was still weighing heavily upon us. Roger asked Amado what this could possibly mean.

"Well, my friend, congratulations! You have just received the highest initiation that the Andes offers, the Initiation of the White Alpaca. Did you feel a rush of energy go into you as the baby released his last breath? In our tradition, this was a gift to you by Spirit."

That certainly put things in a different light. Roger grew up on a farm in the Great Plains of the U.S. and has always had a very special connection with the animals. Given the opportunity, animals would just come over and lean against him. It was funny to see.

Over the next few weeks this kind of got to be a problem. Everywhere we went white animals of all kinds—llamas, alpacas, sheep—would mob Roger. They would be nibbling at his shoes trying to stick their noses in his pockets, breaking away from their owners and running over to him. The owners would run over apologizing, scolding their animals for running off, saying they didn't know what had come over the animal—*he doesn't normally do this*. But we knew what it was . . . .

****

After Roger's coca leaf reading, I had mine. One of the things I spoke to Amado about was the problems I was having with my son, looking for some guidance.

"I just don't get it, he is such a smart kid, why is he doing this stuff?"

"No, he isn't." said Amado.

"What? What did you say?"

"No, he isn't smart. If he was smart, he wouldn't be getting into all this trouble. He might be very intelligent, but he's obviously not very smart."

Oh, boy! I was really liking this guy! What kind of guy is going to tell the mother of someone who has just said that her son is smart, that he isn't??

****

When our 10 weeks was finished in Peru, Jesse, Roger and I went back to the United States. It appears that the idea to bring Jesse to Peru was a good one. He reenrolled in high school and did a complete turnaround. Jesse finally agreed to move in with me and the following quarter he managed to get such good grades in school that he was on the Honor Roll!

Surrender -
Did I Ever Really Have a Choice?

People ask me all the time how I ended up in Peru. The best answer that I've come up with is, "It's just where I'm supposed to be." It is kind of like Peru "claimed" me. I love to travel and immerse myself in different cultures. Over the five years that I kept finding myself coming back to Peru, I must admit I was also wondering to myself "Why Peru? There are so many other countries out there that I could be exploring. This is getting to be a bit embarrassing. Surely I can come up with somewhere different to go. There's Bolivia, Ecuador, Chile, Argentina, and Colombia which I have not yet visited. What's wrong with Indonesia? So many other fascinating places to visit."

But Peru kept calling me back. I am not the only one with this affliction. I know many people who have come to Peru for a visit and either never leave, or go back home and sell everything they own so that they can move back permanently. When people ask us what we're doing in Peru, the most common answer, and one which has become completely acceptable is "I don't know." Then there is the knowing chuckle from those of us who have found ourselves in the same situation.

I had never been particularly interested in history and yet Peruvian history fascinates me. It is completely inexplicable. My bookcase is packed with books written by the first literate chroniclers about the Inka Empire and many of the pre-Inkan civilizations. I just can't get enough of it!

Another theory, one that particularly appeals to me, has to do with the consciousness of the earth itself, sometimes referred

---

[5] Kundalini is described within Eastern spiritual traditions as an indwelling spiritual energy that can be awakened in order to purify the subtle body of a being

to as Gaia. I had read books that maintained that Mother Earth has her own consciousness. They claimed that Mother Earth's kundalini[5] had recently moved. They said that one point of her kundalini is at the center of the earth, and that for the past several thousand years the other point has been in the Himalayas. This is one reason why so many deeply spiritual practices have come out of that area in the past several thousand years. They said that the Himalayas emanate a masculine energy which is one of the reasons that our world has been so dominated by masculine based ideas and concepts.

They said that starting in the 1980s, over a period of years, Mother Earth's kundalini had relocated itself into the Andes Mountains of South America, near the border between Chile and Peru. Because of this we should be entering into a time where the qualities and tendencies of the divine feminine are going to be increasing in the world.

Well, whatever it is that called me to Peru, it is much bigger than me. All I know is that when I'm in Peru I'm happy.

I really like being happy.

Not to say that living in Peru doesn't have its frustrations, because it certainly does. But whenever I leave Peru I usually feel "out of sorts" and apprehensive. When I come back to Cusco and the plane lands on the ground I feel like I am "home", and in the taxi ride from the airport I cannot stop myself from smiling.

It is so inexpensive to live in Peru that although I am not retirement age, I have been able to semi-retire. My hard-earned savings from years of nearly working myself to death in the real estate industry (before it changed so dramatically), carry me a whole lot further than they ever could in the United States.

When I live in the United States I feel like an economic slave.

This one is really key for me. Everything is so expensive and the social standards are so high that I find myself in a position of doing work that I don't really want to do to support a lifestyle that I don't enjoy.

At the time of this writing (2015) it is possible to live in Cusco for $500 per month, if you drop your standards to those that Peruvians find acceptable. I reckon just owning a car in the United States costs about $500 per month minimum, between payments, insurance, gasoline, maintenance, registration, etc. In Cusco I don't even have to own a car. Taxis are cheap, the equivalent of one dollar to go anywhere in the center of town.

I can live what is perceived as a fairly extravagant lifestyle in Cusco for $1000 per month. The longest it takes to get anywhere in the city is 15 minutes. I do not miss the 45 minute commute to and from my work in the U.S. at all.

Those are the practical reasons why I decided to move to back to Peru. But, like I said, those were convenient facts and figures that supported my decision to move to Peru once I got my children launched.

To be frank, I can't remember exactly when the decision came. It was like there was an invisible cord between me and Peru and it was just a matter of time before it pulled me over.

There were people in my life that were not happy with this decision. The next step for most people my age in our society is to wait for their children to marry and have children so that they can become grandparents. My spirit just wasn't ready to settle down into that life.

It took a few years to get the support from those people that didn't agree with my choices. In truth, I believe that this choice on my part was an act of love. It was loving myself enough to follow my spirit. I truly believe that it was loving my children enough to be willing to do this in spite of society disagreeing with my unwillingness to conform to the social customs of people my age. I wanted to be happy rather than die a slow death by living an unfulfilled life, as unfortunately, I watched happen to my mother.

As soon as I felt that my children were capable of getting along without me I started making plans to move to Peru.

Back to the lesson that I learned that when I follow my spiritual guidance, doors just open up for me. Everything just started falling into place. The pull was so strong that I was willing to move to Peru by myself, without a job or any understanding of how I was going to support myself. As it ended up, Ingrid, one of my best friends in Tampa, who had recently lost her husband and was looking to start a new life, had been trying to move to South America for a couple of years. She had been trying all kinds of avenues to do this but none of them had panned out for her.

One day in late 2010 I said to her, "Well, I am moving to Peru next year and you are welcome to come with me." And that was that. She started packing her bags right away!

My South African friend, Lesley (the owner of Casa de la Gringa, where my previous group had stayed while we were in Cusco), and I had stayed in touch during this time and she had come to visit me a couple of times in Florida. Lesley and two partners had been working on renovating a 16th century Spanish colonial house to turn into a boutique hotel the last time I was in Cusco.

One day I received an email from her asking me if Ingrid and I would be interested in helping to manage the new boutique hotel that they had opened. And just like that, we had employment.

I love it when this stuff happens!!

One morning in my meditation, as I was preparing to move to Peru, I got this message:

Lisa, you have a gift. You should share this gift. You know Cusco and the Sacred Valley well, you speak enough Spanish to do this. There are people that would like to go to Peru that will never go by themselves. You need to offer to take them to Peru.

Wow! In addition to preparing to move myself to Peru I found myself organizing and eventually taking a group of 12 people with me. It was an amazing experience. I got to share this with my sister, her daughter and her daughter's fiancé, and several of my friends.

Ingrid was gung ho to move to Peru with me. I didn't know how she was going to react to the high altitude, and with my experiences in the past with altitude issues and my friends, my one request of Ingrid was that she come on this tour with us to be sure she was going to be okay and happy.

The group stayed in Cusco for 12 days and we had an amazing time. Peru has a way of sometimes changing people and my friends were over the moon with their experiences. I got to share my new home with my sister, which meant so much to me. They went back home, and Ingrid and I stayed on a couple of weeks longer, a total of a month. During this time we found an apartment and the basic necessities to live there.

We both then went back to the U.S. for a month and parted with our belongings. I left my three-bedroom house and all its contents with my daughter—they were hers as long as she just paid the mortgage, which was lower than any apartment she could find in a decent part of town. I found her roommates whose rent would pretty much cover the expenses. And within a month, Ingrid and I were living in Cusco.

Part 2

An Insider's Guide to the Andean Culture

Beautiful Cusco

As the plane was coming in for a landing, I was filled with joy. The Cusco Valley is surrounded by high mountains so the descent into Cusco is pretty dramatic. The plane flies over and past Cusco and then banks heavily to one side. Out one window you see the ground below, while on the other side of the plane, you are looking straight up into outer space. It makes your heart lurch and pound, and there are many white knuckles clenching the armrests.

I didn't care! I was so freakin' happy to be finally achieving my goal of six years—finally moving to Peru and starting a new life! The plane leveled out and approached the runway to make its landing. We were about 20 feet off the ground when I suddenly felt as if a giant ball of energy dropped out of my body and sunk itself into the Earth. It was a very strange sensation! I looked at Ingrid and said, "I think I have just been planted!"

All smiles in the taxi to our apartment, we were overjoyed to be starting our new lives at last! The next days were filled with trying to furnish our apartment and stock our kitchen. At the time, Cusco had no department stores, (though now it has a mall!) so we were running all around to the markets and little shops trying to find things, setting up utilities, buying furniture, etc. It was a very busy time!

Within a week, we were starting our new jobs!

****

Cusco is a very pretty city. In the 1400s, it was the spiritual center of the Inka Empire. It was well laid out in the shape of a puma, in alignment with the celestial bodies and constellations. Instead of paying taxes in currency, the population had to devote time to helping build the Empire, so there was no shortage of manpower. They built temples and palaces and some of the most phenomenal stonework man has ever created.

The Inka did not have a monetary system. Gold and silver were used to represent the divine masculine and feminine, and the Q'oricancha or Sun Temple was actually sheathed in gold when the Spanish arrived in 1532.

During their conquest, the Spanish changed much of Cusco's appearance and culture. Of course, all of the Inkan gold and silver sacred objects disappeared as they were melted down and made into coins to ship back to Spain. The Spanish also reconfigured much of the city. Now Cusco is a beautiful combination of austere, imposing Inka stonework and pretty Spanish plazas with their beautiful arches and cathedrals.

Cusco is interesting—geographically, it is not really a very large town. One of the great attractions for me about living in central Cusco was that I didn't have to own a car. Taxis were cheap and if you couldn't find a taxi for some reason or the roads were blocked off (which they frequently were, and without warning, due to road works or constant celebrations), you could always walk home if you lived near the center. So with the population density being fairly high and the actual size of the town being fairly small, things are quite close together, in easy walking distance. There is a lot of life in the streets. Cusco is vibrant, full of life, and if you are walking from one place to another, you will most likely run into people you know. This makes for lovely social opportunities.

Another thing that I love about the culture is the concept of the plazas. There are many plazas where people can meet and socialize. The traditional Peruvian culture does not allow for personal space at home. Most areas of the house, including bedrooms are shared with other family members. Frequently there are several generations living in the same house, as well as children that have been taken in by the family from other family members. In some homes I was in, additional children kept turning up, and when I asked the other children who they were or what their relationship was to the family, they didn't know. So home is more for family, and when they want other company besides their family, most of the time they go out. They go out into the street where there is so much life and vibrancy. And they go to the plazas.

The plazas have park benches and fountains and you'll frequently see lovers on the park benches in what appears to be the most intimate of moments. The people practice their dance steps for the upcoming festivals in the smaller plazas, accompanied by someone playing a flute or drum. You see every age of people doing this, from four year olds to adults. I love walking past these dance practices! It fills my heart so much sometimes it feels like it will burst! What a wonderful way to spend your time–dancing!

Peru is very near the equator. This means that there is not much variance during the year in the time when the sun rises and sets. It only varies from one part of the year to the next by about a half hour. The sun rises between 5:00 and 5:30 in the morning, and sets between 6:00 and 6:30 in the evenings. Consequently, they do not observe daylight savings time. I was amazed to find that Machu Picchu is considered "tropical", even though it is at 8600 feet above sea level and is very chilly in the mornings before the sun burns off the mists and clouds. Indeed, ferns and orchids grow there!

The population of the entire district of Cusco in 2013 was 1.3 million people, though the city of Cusco is only 450,000. It does not have the big city feel. It is fairly compact and seems to have all of the advantages of a big city, and fewer of the disadvantages than most cities its size. At the peak of the Inka Empire, the population of Cusco was thought to be around 300,000, though after the Spanish conquest it had dwindled down to 40,000. So many died from disease brought in by the Europeans, not to mention the death toll from their own civil war just prior to the arrival of the Spanish. The dominant languages are Spanish and Quechua (73% speak Spanish and 24% speak Quechua.) In southern Peru, Quechua is predominant in the countryside.

There is a mountain to the south of Cusco, called *Araway Qhata* (closest translation would be "Hangman's Slope") where huge letters have been carved into the side of it that are redefined annually which say *Viva El Peru* (Long live Peru). I had a perfect view of it from my bedroom window. Just behind it is the curved peak of the mountain they call Mama Simona. She is the guardian *apu* of Cusco (actually, because she is considered feminine, she is technically called a *ñusta*, the Quechua word for princess.)

Tourism is big business, which means that you are more likely to find English-speaking Peruvians in Cusco than in some other parts of Peru, though certainly not a majority. Ninety-nine percent of tourists who come to Peru come to Cusco. Tourism is the #2 industry in Peru, and it is #1 in Cusco.

Cusco seems to also somehow have a magnetic connection for the alternative crowd of foreign travelers who had planned to come to Cusco for a short visit and ended up staying much longer. As a result, it tends to have a cosmopolitan feel to it and a fairly large population of non-Peruvians and expatriates. It's as if just the fact that you are in Cusco means that you already have something in common with other foreigners. It is not uncommon to see 20-somethings hanging out with 50-somethings.

Cusco seems to be a magnet for a certain type of people. For one thing, you have to be relatively healthy to be living at 11,000 feet above sea level. Cusco wasn't really that well-known as a tourist destination, though I do think this is changing. Most people just find themselves in Cusco because they have to go through Cusco to get to Machu Picchu, which has now been named one of the new Seven Wonders of the World.

The first and second times I came to Peru (when I was considering moving there permanently) I would look at the little, brown Quechua mamitas with their long black braids and I thought, "I will never fit in with these people." And it was true, a gringa here will always be a gringa. There is a lot of class division and racism. However, I was pleasantly surprised to find out that this actually worked to my advantage. There is the downside of frequently being seen as a source of income, since we do tend to have more money than the native people. It does get on one's nerves after a short while. I eventually learned to just completely ignore the hawkers with their constant barrage of attempts to sell me massages, silver jewelry, dolls, and Peruvian hats. I just avoid eye-contact, look down and keep walking, or if seated in a plaza, I just close my eyes, and they will wander off. But there are advantages to being a gringa as well. If you are looking for a non-Peruvian friend in a crowd, it is much easier to spot him/her. The indigenous women are short and round. They are considered to be an extension of Pachamama, a part of Mother Earth. All my life I wanted to be a little bit taller and a little bit thinner and in Peru, relatively speaking, I was both. Someone once said to me, "I never thought being a gringa in Peru would put me in a position of privilege . . . but I kinda like it!" Yeah, I shared that sentiment.

Peruvian history goes back thousands and thousands of years. What most people think of when they think of Peru is the Inka, whose peak was about 500 years ago. Most people don't realize that the Inka Empire was created by the assimilation of hundreds of other pre-Inka civilizations with very distinct cultures. Northern Peru has its own fascinating and very distinct history predating the Inka by thousands of years. Naturally, the people from the coast who live in a hot and dry climate (as much of the Peruvian coast is a most unusual combination of sand and cacti, right up to the water's edge), are going to be quite different from the people who live in the mountains or jungle, all of which Peru has.

It is difficult and perhaps not fair to generalize. But as an example, if you look at the historical evidence as depicted in ceramics and art (prior to the Spanish conquest, the Peruvians did not have a written language so there is no written historical record) you will find that the Mochican culture, centered around Trujillo on the northern coast, depicted just about every facet of life and of their culture in ceramics. Therefore, we know more about the Mochican culture than we do most of the other pre-Inka cultures. If you go to the Larco Museum in Lima you will find that they have over 40,000 original Mochican ceramic pieces to see. At the back of the museum is a separate building specifically dedicated to the erotic art ceramics of the Mochican culture. You can actually see many of these pieces online if you do a search for Mochican erotic ceramics or Larco Museum. Let me tell you, they were certainly very creative and uninhibited in the erotica that they produced.

Peruvians are very different from Westerners, which I found very refreshing. They tend to be much more heart-centered rather than mind-based. Because in Hispanic cultures there is so much more life on the street, there are many more opportunities to make contact with people. One thing I noticed is that in Peru people are much more likely to make eye contact with you than they are in the Western cultures. Not in a confrontational or predatory kind of way, but just in noticing that you are there and perhaps acknowledging your existence. As a social creature, there is something very affirming about this sort of behavior.

Life in the Clouds - High Altitude Living

I am writing this chapter to address the questions that many people ask me, and to share a bit of what I have learned in the years of living at high altitudes. People ask me all the time about these things, and I haven't seen it written all in one place before, so this is my offering to those of you who may come to visit.

I LOVE the energy of these magnificent mountains! It is not something that I can describe well, but it feels like they feed me—nourish my body and spirit. There is a quality to the light that is bright, pure, clear, and crisp. The colors have a depth that is so beautiful— the reds, yellows, and oranges just pop!

These are the differences and challenges that one may find when spending time at altitudes of over 10,000 feet above sea level.

Let's talk about the weather at this high altitude, as it appears to be something that is so hard for people to "get." People coming to the high Andes seem completely befuddled (sometimes even offended!) by the weather. They seem to think they should be able to look out the window and predict the weather for the day and how they should dress for it. Not so!

This is key to understanding the weather in the high Andes:

No matter what you see now, it will likely change within the hour.

The weather is extremely CHANGEABLE! You have to be prepared for everything, all the time!

There are two seasons: dry season and rainy season. Within those two seasons, there are a couple of months each where there is a better likelihood of the seasons living up to their names, but most of the time it is a roll of the dice.

Rainy season is technically from mid-November to mid-April, but these past few years have been off by as much as two months. Rainy season is about 10°F warmer than dry season, and it is still quite cold at night, usually in the 40s. Of course, it is a bit more humid. It also hails frequently in these high mountains.

The month that it rains off and on every day is February. It is safe to say that it WILL rain in February much of the time. The ground becomes very muddy and saturated, and there are many landslides out in the countryside. Lots of tour companies just shut down for February since it can be a dangerous time to travel. This is also summer break for the kids from school, from Christmas to the beginning of March. (In the Southern Hemisphere, the seasons are reversed from the Northern Hemisphere.) Many people head for the coast during this time, where it is hot.

As a side note: In Peru, people from the mountains (they call them *Serranos* since they are from the *Sierras*) have a reputation for ALWAYS having a jacket with them, and they are usually wearing it. When they go to the hot coastal desert towns, they can't seem to break this habit; it is so deeply instilled in them. The coastal people tease them and shake their heads at how ludicrous it is to have a jacket in their hot climate. In Cusco, it is not unusual for everyone to be wearing their jackets, zipped up to their necks, when they come over to visit, on the buses with closed windows, when they are in their offices, at a concert—ALL THE TIME. It always looked like they were just about to leave! I would say, "Please! Take off your jacket and stay a while!" They will only do so very reluctantly. It seemed it didn't matter what you were wearing underneath that jacket because nobody was ever going to see it!

Another interesting note: August 1st through 12th are called *Las Cabañuelas*. August 1st is Pachamama Day and the day is dedicated to honoring and "feeding" Mother Earth by having *despacho* ceremonies (also known as *pagos* or "payments"–more detail on this in the chapter *The Andean Spiritual Path*)) as an Offering to Mother Earth in hopes of encouraging her to bring them good weather and harvests in the year to come. Each day represents a month of the year, and the farmers watch the weather intently during these 12 days to predict what it will do in the year to come, and they plant their crops accordingly. (The Spanish brought this tradition with them when they came.) Much of Peru is an agrarian culture, and rainfall is extremely important because much of the land does not have manmade irrigation systems.

Back to the weather: Dry season is technically from mid-April to mid-November. It very rarely rains in June and July, but they are the coldest months. It is cold at night, frequently very near to freezing. But in the daytime, the sun comes out and warms things up nicely.

The really big difference is whether the sun is out or not.

I have never been to a place where the sun feels so delicious! When the sun is out, you can bask in the glory of its beautiful warm rays, though within 15 minutes, once you have warmed your bones, it becomes too hot, and your skin starts to burn. If you step into the shade, you feel the difference immediately—the air is dry and thinner, and it doesn't hold the heat. Within two or three minutes you are probably cold again. If a cloud passes in front of the sun, you find yourself ferreting around for your jacket or sweater. Once you've been through this process for a few days, it is very easy to understand why the Inka worshipped the sun. The sun changes everything.

There is a saying that goes like this:

Cielo Serrano, lagrimas de mujer,

Y cogera de perro, no has de creer!

Andean Sky, a woman's tears,

A limping dog, you should never believe!

(It rhymes in Spanish)

67

Basically, they are saying to never trust an Andean sky (or a woman's tears or a limping dog).

The good news is that, though the weather is so changeable, Cusco does not have extreme shifts in temperature that many places do. When it is cold, it usually stays in the 30F's, if it dips below freezing, it is just barely, and it will warm up within hours. Even when the sun is fierce, it only gets into the 80Fs, so you only have people with heat-stroke if they are over-exerting themselves and don't have the sense to stop and take a break in the shade.

Consequently, it is the custom not to use heat or air conditioning in the high Andes, though as a tourist you can find it in some luxury hotels. Admittedly, part of the reason for this is financial, but most of it is because that's just the way it has always been and that is what they are accustomed to (though I hear that natural gas is making its way to Cusco soon.) They believe it is unhealthy to use a heater and to not have a flow of fresh air passing through a room, and perhaps they are right.

In the U.S. & Europe the generally accepted temperature indoors is between 68F and 78F. I lived in an apartment in Cusco that got a lot of sun (which is hard to find!), and the average temperature in my apartment was 58F-62F. I went for months at a time without seeing my naked skin because it was just too cold. Unless you are in the sun, going sleeveless is highly unlikely. If you descend into the Sacred Valley, as much as 3,000 feet, this changes, and you can wear lighter clothes during the day as long as you have some sort of wrap for when the sun disappears behind a cloud or you go indoors.

Alpaca wool fascinates me! It seems to "breathe"—it is usually warm enough and yet not too hot. It is perfect for this climate. Alpaca fleece is very fine, light, and luxurious. It is durable, soft, thermal, and also water-repellent. While it is similar to sheep's wool, it is warmer and not prickly. It has no lanolin, which makes it hypo-allergenic.

You need layers: A lightweight shirt or t-shirt, with a sweater on top and access to a jacket or wrap of some kind, nothing too heavy unless it is night time in June or July. You need something waterproof, like an umbrella or your jacket, and also a hat and sunglasses. If you are going to be exposed to the elements and sun, you also need sun-block and a waterproof poncho. You probably should carry a bottle of safe drinking water.

Now let's talk about high altitude living. I would like to say that my reason for sharing this is not to put anyone off coming to the high mountains. However, if you have health issues that involve your lungs, or heart or have high blood pressure, you should definitely check with your doctor. I have worked in tourism for years and I have seen a lot. I understand that people are really busy and don't have the time or interest to do the research to know about these things in advance. I was exactly the same way. My goal was just to get there, and I would deal with the rest as it came.

This really does deserve more attention than that though. This is not just another vacation destination. One of my pet peeves was people blowing into the hotel where I was working and thinking they could just come screaming in from the airport, drop off their bags and check-in, then meet for a tour of the ruins in 20 minutes. Or thinking they could fly in one day and do a 4-day Inka Trail trek the next day. It really isn't prudent. You need a couple of days to acclimatize!

The first and most obvious indication that you are at a high altitude, which is recognizable within seconds of leaving the pressurized cabin of the airplane, is that there is less oxygen in the atmosphere, resulting in a feeling of lightheadedness as you come down the ramp from the airplane. More red blood cells are required to live in high altitude, to carry more oxygen to your brain. It takes a day or two for your body to get the message and adjust to this dramatic difference in elevation and levels of oxygen in the rarified air. Luckily, when you sleep the first night, your body does a pretty dramatic recalibration and the second day in Cusco is much better. Always take the first day really easy, and nothing too strenuous on the second day. Ninety-five percent of people have no problem adjusting to the high altitude as long as they take it easy the first day. One thing that surprises people is that no one can really tell who is going to not be in that 95%. Being fit is, of course, always helpful, but it is no guarantee. I have seen families land at the airport and the ones in their 60's were fine, but it was the 21 year old runner who found it challenging. Obviously, there are a few clear indicators. If you need to carry around an oxygen bottle with you at sea level, you should probably not go to the mountains.

But about 5% of people take longer than this to acclimatize. Conscious deep breathing helps dramatically, and failing that, you can purchase cans of oxygen in any pharmacy. One or two breaths of oxygen can make all the difference in the world. You feel it immediately.

Of course, any physical exertion whatsoever is felt instantly with breathlessness and a pounding heart. Anything over 10,000 feet above sea level is considered "very high altitude" and one must be sure that he/she can handle it. Any lung condition, even a case of pneumonia in the past, can have a huge influence on how you adapt to this high altitude.

Other things that short-term tourists notice are:

- Slowing of metabolism resulting in:
  o A decrease in appetite
  o An increase in how quickly alcoholic beverages affect them

- Nose bleeds and runny nose, frequently due to the drier air

- More sun sensitivity. The atmosphere is thinner, and the sun is brighter. Sunglasses, hats, and sunblock are absolutely essential!

On rare occasions, it is possible to have difficulty sleeping. Or perhaps you might wake up in the night with a "start", which is usually an indication that you are not breathing deeply enough, and your oxygen level has dropped to the point it has awakened you. Usually sitting up and taking 20 deep breaths or a couple of shots of the canned oxygen will remedy this.

If one does not get enough oxygen to the brain they will get a splitting headache. If it is ignored, things can get much worse. It is no joke. Listen to your body. Take it easy for the first couple of days. It makes all the difference in the world.

There are medications available if you find you are one of the few who are affected by high altitude sickness. In Peru, they call it *soroche*. You can buy *soroche* medication in any pharmacy. It is a combination of caffeine and aspirin, and it opens up the capillaries in your brain to allow more blood to flow. Outside of Peru (it wasn't available in Peru at the time of this writing) you can buy Diamox (Acetazolamide) which increases the oxygen in your blood, but you must start taking it two days before you reach a high altitude. It won't help you if you are already having problems. It also has side effects that can be challenging for some.

The best solution is coca leaves!! The mountain people have been using them for thousands of years, and they are extremely effective! They are also very nutritive and help in digestion. They are good for your teeth, and contrary to all the propaganda, they do not make you high in any way if taken alone. If you want a buzz from them, you have to use a catalyst which is usually available where you buy the leaves, called *llipta* (pronounced yipta) which is a vegetal ash/lime. It is a nasty black paste, and you put a little of it with the coca leaves and stash the leaves down in your cheek, biting down on them occasionally. I prefer to use bicarbonate of soda (baking soda) which has the same effect and doesn't burn a hole in my cheek. The effects last about 45 minutes and are similar to caffeine. It opens up the capillaries to allow more oxygen to the brain and lifts your spirits a little. It also takes away tiredness, hunger, and is a mild stimulant, so like coffee and tea, you don't want to use it after 5 or 6 p.m.

My only caveat to using coca leaves if you are not accustomed to using them is to be sure that boiling water is used to make your coca tea, to kill any germs that may accompany them, just as you would be careful in eating any unwashed fruits or vegetables. When the leaves are harvested, they are laid out on the ground in the sun to dry. Chickens and other animals may walk on top of them and leave bacteria that you don't want to ingest.

Those of us who choose to stay a bit longer in Cusco learn that all kinds of other things are affected by high altitude living.

Understanding this helps a lot: as altitude increases, the atmospheric pressure decreases, thus there is not as much external pressure placed on objects at higher altitudes. Believe it or not, this even affects the temperatures at which water boils.

Per my calculations, water boils at 212°F (100°C) at sea level. At 11,000 feet, water boils at closer to 190°F, and at 15,000 feet, it is closer to 180°F. This affects all kinds of things. If you want to kill the nasty critters that could be in your drinking water, fewer of them die at 180°F than die at 212°F, so you have to boil the water for longer if you want to make it safe for drinking. Of course, water cannot get any hotter than its boiling point, no matter how long you heat it.

You also have to extend your cooking times when using water. So a three-minute egg is no longer a three-minute egg. Cooking with oil and microwaves are apparently not affected in the same way.

Also, at higher altitudes humidity tends to decrease as the rate of evaporation speeds up. This dries out your skin, the inside of your nose, mouth, eyes, and any food you are cooking. During dry season, I cannot wear my contact lenses for as long as I can in rainy season, and every morning I wake up with scales inside my nostrils. Leaving a bowl of water in the room or running a hot shower will help increase the humidity.

Some people find the dryness a relief to humidity. They say that it opens up their breathing. If you have oily skin, sweating can exacerbate acne or pimples and some people find their complexion is better in the dry air.

This is also one of the reasons that spicy sauces are popular. They make your nose run and make you sweat. Liquor also warms you up, and there is plenty of that available!

Gases expand more quickly at higher altitudes. They do not eat many beans up there for a reason! It took me years to figure out that I had to completely eliminate broccoli, cabbage, beans and other gassy foods from my diet if I wanted a social life at all or wanted to sleep at night. (!!!)

As a result of the higher expansion of gasses, when you are baking you have to reduce your leavening. Because the atmospheric pressure is less and hence the air is thinner, this allows dough to rise too quickly. Additional liquid is usually needed because the flour tends to dry out in low humidity areas. You need more moisture-retaining agents. Cooking times or temperatures will also need to be reduced when baking, or the food will be burnt on the outside and not cooked through on the inside! This has resulted in many cakes collapsing–an ongoing frustration for my baking buddies!

It is something you have to play with and get used to! My first attempt at making brownies to take to a Thanksgiving dinner ended up in a disgusting goo that was inedible—and that was following the high altitude directions on the box!

I had three computers crash in three years as a result of the difference in air pressure. The hardrive disks on most computers spin and the space between the spin and the reader of the disk is very finely calibrated. Because of the difference in air pressure, the tiniest change in this space can cause a computer's hard-drive to crash. I eventually had to get a solid-state hard-drive for my computer, which has no moving parts.

The good news is that not so many things can live at high elevations. There are fewer insects, reptiles, rabies and bacteria. The bad news is that we tend to heal more slowly at higher elevation.

The trick is to not get sick to begin with, especially with colds. They easily turn into bronchial problems or pneumonia pretty quickly. At sea level I was used to healing myself within a week of a cold. After 10 days in Cusco, I would end up at my doctor's office again and again, my normal remedies were not working. He would say to me, "Lisa, why do you wait so long to come see me?!" I was used to healing myself. In the end, I became very serious about avoiding people with colds!

People who are moving to Cusco and the Sacred Valley frequently ask me what the most important items are to bring with them, so I will also use this opportunity to share this information here.

Keeping in mind that since I have never lived in a really cold environment before, staying warm and comfortable is paramount to me. My most valued items were my down comforter (the blankets here are super heavy! We call them "bone-crushers"), a good quality hot water bottle (they are available but are low quality and don't last long before they start to leak), heavy thermal socks, and quality thermal underwear. Finding quality goods in a developing country can be a challenge. As I walk through the stores and markets, it occurs to me that what they send to Peru is what nobody in a first world country would touch with a 10-foot pole—they are SO ugly!

Towels, sheets, undergarments, and socks are usually what I bring back when I visit the U.S. Also, vitamins and supplements are not readily available. Again, Cusco seems to be coming up in the world, and with a new mall (they even have a multiplex movie theater now!) and an international airport under construction, we all expect this to change in the next several years.

The mail service is not reliable, so ordering from the Internet doesn't really work.

Bring anything that will make you really happy and comfortable. You do NOT need to bring sweaters! There are gorgeous and fairly inexpensive sweaters made from alpaca wool here. Chocolate here is also excellent and plentiful (REALLY good news!) though it is not cheap. Peru has some of the best natural produce I have ever eaten in my life!

Those are the things that we learn to live with. The truth is that in spite of all of the challenges, there are many of us who are madly in love with these Peruvian mountains!!

Peruvian Food

In my humble opinion, food is one of Peru's most wonderful offerings! It absolutely shines in this area. The climate of Peru is very diverse. It has an incredible variety of microclimates between its high mountains, coastal deserts and jungles. Peru has 28 of the world's 32 climates within its borders.

The produce is so abundant, so full of energy and life, and so incredibly yummy!! GMOs are outlawed in Peru. Much of the produce comes from individual farmers who work the land with their hands and animals. You see very little machinery as you go through the countryside.

The markets are like your own personal horn of plenty! You will see fruits and vegetables here that you probably have never seen elsewhere. It is an absolute feast for the senses! My own personal favorites are the mangoes and the avocados. I have never had them so delicious in the U.S. or Europe! There is a plethora of fresh herbs for making tea or for healing. Fresh chamomile and lemon grass for teas are very common.

And the potatoes!! There are over 3,000 varieties of potatoes in Peru! I actually have become intimidated in the potato aisle at the market and walked away with nothing–I was overwhelmed by the choice! (I have since learned to just ask the people which to use to fry, to boil, or for soup, etc.)

There are yummy, moist yellow potatoes, white potatoes, tiny black ones, purple-skinned ones shot through with purple colored designs inside... My very favorites are the potatoes brought to me by my Q'ero *compadre*, Juan, which he has grown way up in the mountains on his land in Q'eros with his own hands and love. I can eat two or three of these gorgeous, little potatoes, and they are so full of energy that I can't eat another bite!

It is very easy to be a vegetarian or vegan in Cusco. There are many restaurants catering to dietary restrictions, and any regular menu normally has plenty of dishes to choose from. One of my favorites is the *cremas*. These are soups that are made from fresh vegetables and then pureed. Despite the name, they usually do not have any dairy products in them. Most places offer *crema de zapallo,* my personal favorite, which translates to "pumpkin soup." But it isn't really pumpkin. There is a squash in Peru that is the size of a watermelon and resembles a giant acorn squash. The inside color is yellow, and they boil it down until it is a magnificent mush, then flavor it. You can also get *cremas* of asparagus, mushroom, corn, and other vegetables.

There are so many different varieties of grains, it is amazing! Of course there are wheat and oats. And most people these days are familiar with quinoa, which has the highest protein of any grain, is gluten-free and makes a delicious soup. There are many varieties of quinoa, including black and red. They frequently use it to make desserts—I had quinoa ice cream once! They even make a risotto out of quinoa, which they refer to as "quinotto".

But there is also *kiwicha* (amaranth) and *kañiwa,* a relative of quinoa. Maca is a relative of the radish and the dried root is pulverized and sometimes used in baking. *Tarwi* is the seed of the lupin plant and flower, which is more like a bean or seed and is ground into a paste or eaten whole. It resembles small, white lima beans. In truth, none of these is technically a grain, but they are used as we use grains. They are readily available in the markets, either whole, or ground into flour which can be used in baking. They also make flours out of potato.

There are so many healthy options for food in Peru! The markets in Peru put the produce department of our Western grocery stores to shame.

Peruvian cuisine has gained popularity in the world. As a matter of fact, Peru has been recognized twice in a row recently by the World Travel Awards as the top pick for traveling gourmands in search of delicious food.

A few of the most popular Peruvian dishes are the following:

Lomo Saltado

Peru has some unusual historical ties with the people from China and Japan which is best exemplified in this dish. It is considered to be Asian-fusion cuisine. It is a stir-fry of tenderloin of beef, onions and fresh tomatoes served with a soy sauce over white rice and topped with fried potatoes. It is on most menus and super savory!

Trout

The coasts of Peru have incredible seafood. If you are living in the highlands the only fresh fish you are likely to find is trout, which lives in lakes and is also farmed. The trout in Peru is more like salmon–it is orangey-pink and very meaty and succulent.

Aji (pronounced *ah-hee*)

Though I am not too crazy about peppers, I mention this because aji is the most popular and frequently used chili in Peru. It is a bright orange chili with a fruity taste, very flavorful, and has a medium to hot heat, which can be toned down in various ways.

Ceviche

Ceviche is a treat for most Peruvians. It is raw fish that has been marinated in citrus juice. The citric acid cooks the fish, giving the fish a delicate flavor and a slightly chewy consistency. It is usually spiced up a bit with red onion and aji pepper. This is usually eaten at lunchtime as, especially in the higher altitudes, people pay careful attention to their digestion. Different types of fish are prepared this way, but in the highlands it is usually trout.

Choclo

This is a large kernel corn which is described as chewier, starchier and less sweet than other types of corn. It has a slightly nutty taste and is often served with *paria* cheese, which tastes like a slightly salty, mild feta cheese. The kernels are so big that they are frequently broken off one at a time and consumed as a finger food, rather than bitten off the cob. It is sometimes served with *ceviche* or cut into wheels and makes a beautiful addition to soups. The kernels are also toasted and served salted, kind of like corn nuts.

Chicharron

I really enjoy pork and it took me quite a while to find it in Peru because I didn't know what to ask for. I was looking on the menu for p*uerco (pork) or cerdo (pig).* But in Cusco they call pigs *chancho.* I was very happy to find *chicharron,* which is large chunks of pork that have been deep-fried.

Lechon

Leche is the word for milk, so technically *lechon* should be suckling pig. Sometimes it is, but it is frequently used to describe any roast pork.

Aji de Gallina

This is a rich, velvety stew made with chicken, aji peppers, condensed milk and crushed peanuts, then thickened with white bread and usually served over white rice. This can be a pretty spicy dish, but they can almost always tone it down if you ask

Papas Huancaina

This is basically the vegetarian version of *aji de gallina,* the same lovely sauce served over potatoes. For some reason, this is normally served as an appetizer instead of a main dish.

Chicha Morada

This is a non-alcoholic drink made from Peruvian black or purple corn which has been boiled with pineapple, cinnamon, clove, and sugar. It is an ancient favorite, even pre-dating the Inka Empire. Good chicha morada is really tasty, and bad chicha morada that is poorly flavored and overly sweet tastes like grape Kool-aid.

Alpaca

A steak from the alpaca is a lean meat with a mild taste, a bit like a pork chop. Llama is never served for some reason. I suspect that it is too tough a meat for common consumption. One Quechua word that has made its way into the English language is *jerky*, which comes from the Quechua word *charky,* referring to dried strips of alpaca or llama meat.

Guinea Pig

For reasons that are beyond me, guinea pig–called *cuy* in Peru–is considered a rare and expensive treat which is served on special occasions, similar to the way we serve turkey. It has been a staple in the Peruvian diet for centuries. I have tried it on numerous occasions and, to be honest, it hardly seems worth the trouble. There is so little meat on a guinea pig, so many membranes and it is very greasy. I find it fairly disgusting. The only real meat is on the thigh. It is probably similar to fried rat. If you are really hungry, order something else.

Cuy is so important to Peruvian culture that there is even a painting which is hanging in the Cathedral in Cusco which depicts Christ and the Apostles eating *cuy* at The Last Supper.

****

My only caveat with food in Peru is to be sure that your food is prepared in a place with good hygiene. There are many bacteria in Peru that we are not accustomed to and the standards of hygiene are low. I have watched the *campesinos* in the countryside washing the lettuce that they are harvesting in the snowmelt runoff that the animals traipse through, drink from and occasionally defecate in. In the markets they frequently refreeze what has not sold in a day, sometimes for several days running. They use the same oil for frying for days on end.

The sensible thing to do if you are in Peru for a short period of time is to be sure that you eat in high-quality restaurants and to be sure that your food is well-cooked. Only eat fruits and vegetables that are cooked or can be peeled. Avoid eating food cooked and served on the streets.

Tap water is not suitable for drinking unless it has been boiled first. Bottled water is readily available for purchase just about everywhere.

Taxi Chat

The taxi world, I learned while in Cusco, is a culture unto itself. The first stage in the Taxi Culture life of a Westerner in Cusco is as a tourist. It probably starts at the airport. Once you collect your luggage at Baggage Claim, you are herded out the doors and find yourself outside. There are barricades that separate you from the people who are waiting to meet people arriving into Cusco. The moment you walk through the opening you are bombarded with a wave of taxi drivers.

The first wave of taxi drivers will offer to take you into town for S/30 (30 Soles–at the time of this writing US$1 = S/2.5 to S/3) which seems fairly reasonable to most Westerners. This first wave of taxi drivers will have very nice vehicles, are clean, and are possibly in some kind of uniform, maybe even young and good-looking with cool sunglasses. If you have a ton of luggage you will probably just decide to go with them.

If you walk another 5-10 steps you'll hit the next wave of taxi drivers who will offer to take you into town for S/20.

If you keep walking, some will approach you and ask you how much you want to pay to go into town. You'll probably find yourself at around S/15, maybe a little less.

If you don't have much luggage you can walk right out of the gated airport entrance, out to the right and catch a cab on the main road for S/7 or S/8.

For me to get from my apartment to the airport was S/5 or S/6. Tipping taxi drivers is not customary.

If you read the guide books, they will tell you to never go with a taxi that doesn't have a license displayed. There are people with vehicles in Cusco who will just pick up passengers en route to where they are going. In my experience these guys usually want to overcharge. If I choose to take one of these, I always arrange a price before I step foot into the vehicle. I always look them in the eye and decide if I feel safe going with them.

I have personally never had a bad experience in a taxi in my years in Cusco, but I have heard horror stories.

One person's sister took a cab when she first got in town from the airport to her destination. She quickly ran in to check to be sure she had the right place, and when she came back out, the taxi had gone with all her belongings. One guy I know was drunk at 3:00 a.m. and the taxi driver robbed him on his way home.

I think it pays to know the rules. I have always taken a lot of taxis in Cusco. For one thing, my neighborhood has quite a reputation of territorial dogs that are a problem if they don't know you (see the section on Dogs later in this book). I get around this by always taking the same route in and out of my pedestrian-only neighborhood so all the dogs know me on my route home. After nine or ten at night it is not really safe to be walking around alone. One time I was three blocks from home and thought surely I could get away with it, but there were drunks in the street and so I turned around and walked back and took a taxi (sigh…).

When you are a tourist and don't know where you are going and can't speak the language, you have a very different energy about you than when you live there and know what's what. My goal was to be seen as a local, so that taxi drivers were not constantly trying to take advantage of my gringa self.

Cusqueñeans are extremely polite. When you get in a taxi and shut the door, the first thing you should say is *"Buenos dias," "Buenas tardes"* or *"Buenas noches"* (*noches* is when it is dark). If you hop in the cab and bark an order at the driver, he will wheel his body around, look you in the eye and say, "Buenos dias…" insinuating that you have forgotten your manners. This will not get you off to a good start.

The next thing you need to know is that (at the time of this writing) to go anywhere in the center of town costs S/3. You need to know where the boundaries are, more or less. If you are within the boundaries, which vary depending on where you are coming FROM, the fare is S/3 unless the taxi driver says otherwise before he takes off. If it is raining, or peak travel time, or there is really bad traffic, he will likely try for S/4. But if he doesn't say that upfront, you are justified in just paying S/3. After 9:00 p.m. or 10:00 p.m. the fare goes up to S/4, and after midnight it is S/5.

But this is the trick: you have to have exact change. Getting change in Cusco is always a challenge. I kid you not, I go to my bank and wait as much as a half hour to see a teller to get change. They ALWAYS give me a hard time. I always tell them I will wait, and they go from teller to teller, trying to scrounge up coins for me. It is ridiculous. But having correct change saves me so much in cab fares! It saves in arguments too. If you have exact change, there is usually not an argument, it is worth it to me! (To squirrel away change, always use the biggest bill you can get away with, and if they ask you if you have change, just say "No.")

The next trick is to know the customs that make you look like a local. First of all, you ALWAYS enter the cab on the curb side, never in the middle of the road. They do not want their door ripped off by traffic coming the other direction and the roads are very narrow usually.

You ALWAYS sit in the back, on the opposite side of the driver. If you are a young, pretty, slim blonde–NEVER sit in the front! It is suggestive to them and gringas have a reputation for being "easier" than Peruvians, and sitting in the front may have repercussions you were not expecting. I've heard this story several times.

So you are sitting in the back and you have your exact change in your hand. The next trick is: DO NOT START TO CHAT WITH THE TAXI DRIVER. If he starts to chat with you, you are welcome to respond, assuming you speak Spanish (because I have not met a taxi driver yet who speaks English. If they spoke English, they would not be driving a taxi, but instead be in another profession.)

****

After making this mistake hundreds of times, I am fairly well convinced that taxi drivers have a script that they follow with a gringa in the vehicle. It goes like this:

- "What country are you from?"
- "How long have you been here?"
- "Do you have family here?"
- "Are you married?"
- "Where is your husband/boyfriend from?"
- "Do you have children?"
- "Are they here with you?"
- "What you need is a Peruvian boyfriend."

There are a few variations on this theme, and as you can imagine, it can go all over the place. I have been told everything from "I LOVE you! Please call me. Here is my number," to "Do you have any girlfriends who are in town for a few days that would like a Peruvian boyfriend?"

My girlfriends who have no children are frequently offended by what is considered here to be a perfectly acceptable question in a society that sees motherhood as the natural outcome of any sort of sexual relations, not the very personal conscious choice, as we see it.

My favorite response to this by a girlfriend of mine who, when asked, "Who is going to take care of you in your old age??" was this:

"Oh, that will not be a problem! My husband is 16 years younger than I am." That shuts them up!

The next thing you need to know is how to exit a taxi. Never get out on the side with oncoming traffic. Taxi drivers here are very serious about this, to the point that they sometimes even remove the door handle from that side of the car, so that the only way you can get out on that side is if they open the door for you from the outside.

Always look back behind you into the back seat of the car to make sure you have all of your belongings. If you leave anything behind, you will never see it again. Hand the driver the exact change. If you do not have exact change and forgot to ask before you got in the taxi, before you hand him any money, ask how much it will be (*Cuanto seria?*). Do not be shy to count your change in front of them. They ALWAYS do it, even holding bills up to the light to check for counterfeits (there are plenty.)

As you exit the taxi (or many people exit the taxi and then hand the money through the front passenger window) you hand him the fare and exit the taxi saying, "*Muchas gracias, Señor.*" Manners go a long way here too. Ninety percent of the time that works. Ten percent of the time they try to raise the price and I have to say, "No, Señor, I live here, it is always S/3 to come here," which may or may not work.

Not Planning and Other Tendencies

The truth of the matter is that you will drive yourself crazy if you try to plan things out in Peru the way that we do in other parts of the world. It almost seems as if the Peruvians didn't get the planning gene! It baffled me for some time how it could possibly be that they don't plan. I've been going back and forth to Peru since 2005, and I believe I may have begun to understand why the Peruvians don't plan.

First of all, it doesn't work. It's almost as if there's a Bermuda triangle over Peru that causes plans to just evaporate. Once I understood the history a little bit better, and how many times in the past the Peruvians have completely lost everything they had, it helped me to understand the mentality of immediate consumption that seems to be prevalent there.

The chances of losing what you have are high—if not by theft, being absorbed into the family (which is a common theme), then by government or economic collapse. So, perhaps people are not as motivated to achieve and accumulate as is often seen in many other cultures.

Historically, the Inka were very good at creating surplus and storing the food that they grew to plan for future drought. This made it much easier for the Spanish to conquer the Inka civilization because there was such a surplus of stored food. Well, as history tells us, the Spanish took just about everything from the Peruvians and what they got in return was illness, slaughter, and slavery. So perhaps they lost the motivation to save—to store for the future. What the Peruvians are good at now is immediate consumption. When they have money, they spend it; when they have food, they eat it.

The Spanish had guns, cannons and horses, and there is no doubt about the fact that the Spanish warriors were far better equipped than the Inka. Could it be that all of the Inka that fought were killed, leaving only the more docile people alive and it is only these ancestors who contributed to the current gene pool?

I have pondered why the people are the way they are in the Andes. Could it be in part because they were oppressed for hundreds of years, first by the Inka, and then by the Spanish? The Inka society was very rigidly regulated, which also made it easier for the Spanish to step in and take over. Still, anyone who didn't cooperate was killed. So could it be that the people who survived were not the fighters, but people who were more passive? Perhaps the gene pool of the survivors were gentler and more compliant people who managed to stay alive through the conquest.

People were not encouraged to be free-thinkers or innovative. If they wanted to survive, they were encouraged to be hard-working, to conform and to not make waves. I still see evidence of these preferences in Andean society, though as the world becomes more global in nature, there are exceptions to this, especially in the larger cities.

At one point I began to believe that what I was perceiving as passive in my experiences in Andean society, could also be seen as passive-aggressive. This comes out in what is known in Peru as *envidia* (envy) which is much more pervasive in Cusqueñan society than I have ever seen anywhere else. There is an underlying feeling that "if you have something that means I don't have it"–what I call *scarcity consciousness*, as opposed to *abundance consciousness* or "there is plenty for everyone". I was completely unsuccessful in my attempts to get people that I worked with to consider this mindset or embrace abundance consciousness. In truth, I found it exhausting, and it felt like slamming my head against a brick wall. It is very deeply ingrained in the society.

Generally speaking, the Andean people are not particularly confrontational. Though they have a reputation for being extremely emotional, the mountain people in Cusco (the *Serranos)* are not very demonstrative with their emotions. It has been a survival skill for hundreds of years. Estimates are that as much as 90% of the population of Peru from the 1500s was decimated either by disease—the viruses that the Spanish brought and shared with them, like smallpox and influenza—their own Civil War (which was already in progress when the Spanish arrived) or just poor treatment.

It seems to me that the Andean culture tends to be very people-pleasing, they always want to say "yes" to any and everything you ask of them. There is a 50/50 chance that people will do what they say they are going to do or will be where they say they are going to be, and this is culturally acceptable.

They don't say, "When he comes…."
They say "If he comes…."

You can plan all you want to in Peru, but it isn't going to happen

Learning to live with this has been one of the single most frustrating experiences I have had. After all these years, I still struggle with it, but I have learned a few tricks to surviving in this culture without just setting my hair on fire. What you have to do is to double book everything! It is really quite amazing, but it works. You plan two or three things to happen at the same time, and you can pretty much guarantee that at least one of them is going to cancel, probably two—and maybe all three. But if you only plan one thing at a time, then you spend much of your time disappointed and waiting for something that isn't going to happen.

So you just stop planning. I looked at my calendar earlier in the week and aside from working, there was nothing on my calendar for the week. Did I end up doing nothing? Absolutely not! Things seem to happen much more in the present moment.

Now when I look at my calendar and see these empty blocks, I think to myself, "Wow! I wonder what's going to happen…." It really is a kind of an attitude shift, even a form of surrender, and actually, since I've taken on this attitude my life has unfolded in ways I could have never expected. Life has created a direction of its own, and things seem to happen and manifest themselves. It is really quite liberating!

****

I am told that behavior varies dramatically in different regions. Peru is an incredibly diverse country. The people from the south (which is where Cusco is) are quite different from the people in the north, those who live on the coast, or those who live in the jungle.

Cusqueñeans themselves rely economically very much on tourism, but simultaneously feel invaded by the constant bombardment of people from other places. They are a traditional people and somewhat resistant to change.

The people from Lima, who tend to have much more Spanish influence and thinking than the more indigenous highlanders, see the Cusqueñeans as a pretty closed group. Based on past experience, the Spanish didn't bring much of anything to benefit the Inka, and they came in with an attitude of superiority, which persists today. So the Cusqueñeans close the emotional gate on them, as best they can.

Time and Space

Peruvians have a very different concept of time and space. We all know that Latinos have a reputation for being very *kissy* and *huggy*. When you walk into a room, whether it is business or personal, you go around to each individual and kiss everyone on the cheek, or if you are a man greeting a man, you shake hands. When you leave, even if it is literally five seconds later, there is the same kissing and shaking of hands expected before you depart. They call this *cariño* (affection).

Westerners frequently see this as an invasion of personal space. Peruvians are very family and socially oriented. They tend to share communal space, frequently having no personal space at all, even at home. I found this very hard to get used to at work, where I was used to having my own office, or at least my own desk. How could I possibly get organized with no personal space?! I felt I was expected to *float* around to various locations to whatever location was not in use by someone else and therefore available, and for me to just do my job from there. I had no control at all over my office supplies or if the snacks I brought in would be there next time I needed them. *Where are my cookies?!* This was a huge adjustment for me.

I used public transportation a lot in Peru since I didn't own a car. Peruvians, men especially, are like babies in a moving vehicle (when they are not driving). They fall asleep almost instantly. Occasionally, their head will end up on your shoulder. Seat-belts are not used on public transportation. With the winding roads through the mountains you are constantly being jostled around this way and that. You are right up against the person beside you whether you like it or not–there's no avoiding it.

On more than one occasion it has happened that I was in a colectivo/van going for an hour or two to another town, and the person beside me, once a 13 year old boy, had his elbow resting on my hipbone the whole way! Peruvians are just not bothered so much about personal space and touching.

Traffic. Many Westerners are completely taken aback at the difference in spatial allowances on the road. Peruvians are much better at judging space than we are in the U.S. They literally come within two inches of each other on the road, and yet they almost never have accidents or bump each other. They don't have lanes painted on the road in most places, and everyone just goes wherever it makes sense to go. They are very yielding to each other, and you almost never hear them blasting their horns at each other the way we do in the U.S. if someone dares to get in our path.

When driving in England, you are not supposed to drive in such a way as to cause the other drivers to be required "to change speed or direction." In Peru, it is absolutely not the same. To me it is indicative of the whole general tendency of the society. They just tend to deal with "what is" and yield when it makes sense without getting all worked up and egotistical about it. This is how they survive living in a country where the only thing that is absolutely predictable is that you are not going to be able to predict anything. Especially when it comes to time.

Ah, time. Time is very fluid in Peru, as it is in many Latin American countries. The general understanding is that two hours after the verbally agreed upon time is about right. My dad was in the military, and punctuality is virtually an obsession for me. This does not work in my favor in South America. We gringas laugh at ourselves at our pathetic attempts to be late.

Peruvians live more in the present than any society I have ever seen. What happens in the present moment is far more important than what could possibly be happening in the future, even if it means someone is waiting for you or someone is going to be let down or disappointed because you didn't show up. They are far more relaxed about time and punctuality.

I tried at the hotel I was working at to have quick daily meetings, and it was extremely frustrating! No one wanted to be the first one there, even if I was already sitting there, waiting. They kept strolling by the door and checking to see if everyone else was there before they'd come in. Somebody has to be first! I tried bawling people out for being five minutes late for a 15 minute meeting and I was told by my bosses to "Chill out, this is Peru!" Never in my life had I had a boss tell me to chill out and drop my standards. It always took half an hour to have a 15 minute meeting.

I found this so incredibly frustrating! One day I heard myself say, "I don't understand what the priority is here, but it certainly isn't 'getting things done!'"

I have even heard that this being late all the time is a problem in the universities with exams. Can you imagine turning up late for exams?! The way they deal with this lack of punctuality at doctor's offices is that they just don't set appointments. They just see whoever turns up, and in the order they turn up. It is perhaps the most sensible thing I have seen.

I spent so much time trying to tap into this unspoken but apparently well-understood concept of time. They ALWAYS lie about what time things are going to start. If they say the band starts at 10:00 p.m., it might be 11:30 p.m. I used to beg them, "Please tell me the real time! I am a gringa, and I can't figure this out!" It didn't work. They won't speak of it. Then I got the feeling that the band wouldn't start until enough people were there to justify playing. But no one would come in from the street until they could hear the band was playing! Then, magically, the band would start, the tables and chairs would all be occupied and the dance floor would be packed! Absolutely baffling to me! When I talk to my South American friends about this, they all just chuckle knowingly and shake their heads.

I had an experience with someone who was doing some work for me on my website. Fifty-percent of the time when we had set an appointment to get together he would not show up. I found it so frustrating that I would arrange my schedule around meeting with him and that he would just leave me sitting around waiting, with no regard at all for the fact that I had other things I could be doing if I wasn't waiting for someone who wasn't going to come. It struck me as so inconsiderate! I tried to confirm our appointments. I would call him on the phone, and he would not answer. So I would text him, and he would not answer. I would send him an email and Facebook message, and he still wouldn't answer.

I really couldn't figure out what was so hard about saying, "I am so sorry, but I won't be able to make it." In the meantime, he was probably thinking, "This stupid gringa really can't take a hint."

A defining moment for me was one day when I called him out on it. I said, "If you cannot come, I would really appreciate it if you would just send me a quick text. I am sitting around waiting for you when I could be out doing other things." The look on his face was so revealing. He was an extremely polite and proper young man in every other way.

He looked crestfallen. The polite and optimistic look that had been on his face fell and a look of disappointment and recognition that I was not going to help him "save face" came over him. This is another example of the passivity that permeates the culture. They do not like to be "called out." Politeness is a much higher priority than honesty, and they don't see standing someone up as impolite. It is like there is an underlying feeling of "I can't do this. Please, oh please, do not hold me accountable or hurt my ego."

****

As a result of my continued frustration at trying to wrap my brain around these dramatic differences in the concepts of time and space I developed a new mantra.

It goes like this:

> *I don't know.*
> *I don't understand.*
> *What does it mean?*

I think the best advice I got regarding this was a common saying:

A la vista sera. Queda!

This translates loosely to "When I see you, it will be."

****

The Inka had a very interesting concept of time. Time was not linear for them, but cyclical. Everything had to do with the cycles for planting and harvesting. They didn't have clocks, but followed the shadows made by the sun, which is evidenced in just about everything they built.

They saw the past as something that was in front of you, because it is known, and the future was behind you as you couldn't see it.

Lying, Theft and Dogs

It might seem odd to be writing a story about my love affair with Peru and to have a chapter about all the negative aspects. The truth is, everything and everyone has a down side. If you are in love with a person and have a long term relationship, you are going to eventually learn about that person's weaknesses. Does it change your love for him or her? Well, I suppose it depends on how you handle it. You learn the weaknesses, and then you try to set up your life and environment so that those weaknesses are not triggered.

Knowledge is power. Chances are that in the society in which you live, there are some pretty major challenges that you work around. The difference is that you know what they are, and you behave in such a way to minimize their impact on your life or to completely avoid them. Just walk into any shopping center in the U.S. and everything from the lighting to the music has been arranged from a merchandising standpoint to get you to part with your money. The milk is at the back of the grocery store so that you have to pass by a million temptations in order to get what you want.

We are brainwashed by advertising into thinking that we need whatever products they are selling. They tell you in so many ways that no one will love you if you don't smell a certain way or own certain items. They use psychology which comes at you in a hundred different ways to get you to spend your money.

The less developed countries are not as sophisticated, but in my estimation, it is the same process. You have money, and someone else wants it. You just need to know the system and how to be conscious of what is happening.

I share this information about a country which I love so much, which also has some areas that seriously challenge my ability to love it at times. They may seem pretty dramatic if you are not accustomed to having to deal with them. To me, it is kind of like being in love with an extremely talented and/or charismatic person who has an addiction. Can you learn to live with it? Some choose not to, but many people learn how to do it, and do it with love for themselves and the other.

LYING

"Truth" is also very fluid in Peru. In the world I grew up in, truth was a black and white issue. Once in a while there was a little gray area, but truth was truth.

Not so in Peru. The truth is less black and white than it is gray. You know that saying "Believe half of what you see and nothing that you hear?" I would not be surprised if I found out that it originated in Peru.

People tell you what they think you want to hear whether it has anything to do with reality or not. They call them "white lies." There was even a chapter in one of my workbooks in Spanish classes called "Excuses Cusqueñeans Make"!! The social differences between Peru and the U.S. are made clear in how each country relates to truth. In Peru, the lack of planning, combined with the fluidity of time and truth, create a barrier that prohibits many things from happening accurately or efficiently.

They do not see lying as something that is wrong. Peruvians frequently don't show up when they say they will and just about any excuse will do and is acceptable. Again, there is the assumption that you are going to realize that they are not telling the truth about why they didn't show up for an appointment, come in to work, or don't have the money they owe you. It seems that saving face in the moment is a much higher priority than honesty. The strange thing that I saw was that because they are expecting you to lie, even when you are telling the truth there is the assumption that you aren't. There frequently is no truth at all behind what you are being told. Generally speaking, they are extremely non-committal in most things, and this is well-understood and accepted in the culture.

I took this very personally on more than one occasion. It is just another cultural norm that one has to adjust to if one is going to retain one's sanity and function in this otherwise amazing country.

THEFT

Ay, ay, ay–theft. This is one of the most annoying problems in Peru. One thing I learned early on is that there are many, many pairs of eyes, and there is *always* someone watching. They are watching for two reasons. The thieves are watching, always looking for an opportunity to do what they do. Everyone else is watching to look out for the thieves. There is the assumption that if you are not paying attention that someone is going to relieve you of your possessions. The attitude is that if you were not watching, you were stupid, because surely you knew that someone would take your stuff.

For the most part, the theft is opportunistic. There is very little violent crime, and the thieves are not mean-spirited like in some places where they would take your stuff and then hurt you just out of meanness. Most of the time, you will never even know you have been robbed until after the fact. But there is always someone watching, waiting for you to let your guard down, to be careless or drunk.

HOW TO MINIMIZE YOUR CHANCES OF GETTING ROBBED

The trick is to be tuned in to your surroundings. Still, if you are in the country long enough, you are going to lose something, so I will share some guidelines to minimize your risk, and minimize your loss.

First of all, assume that you are a magnet for the unwanted attention of thieves simply because the truth of the matter is that you have something that they want. Secondly, assume that you are probably not going to know it is happening because they are extremely good at what they do, and they are very smooth.

Carry as little with you as you can get away with. If you have important documents like passports, make photocopies of them and only carry the originals when absolutely necessary, like when you are actually traveling or entering Machu Picchu. Wear a money belt inside your clothes when you are traveling and carry your passport, credit cards and money in it. Wear pants and put the money belt inside your pants. Only access it when you are alone, like in the bathroom. Plan ahead. (Don't wear it under a dress–you can't get to your money belt when you need it without flashing the world–I learned this one the hard way.) Carry only the cash that you think you will need for the day.

Make sure that all your pockets and bags that contain anything valuable have zippers and are zipped shut. If you carry a purse, make sure it has shorter shoulder straps so that you can keep it under your arm, between your arm and your ribs. Hold it tight and make sure the zipper is at the front and not the back. If you have a backpack, do not have anything of value in the little pockets on the outside.

If you are in a crowded place there is probably a thief scanning the scene, looking for his/her next target. Be aware. Just the fact that you are aware and paying attention, combined with how you are carrying yourself, is going to minimize the chances that you will be the chosen victim.

If you are on a crowded bus or in a crowded market, carry your backpack in front of you, not on your back. If you have a shoulder purse with a long strap, swing it around to the front and put your hand over it. If you have a pocket with a phone or cash in it that doesn't zip, put your hand over the opening. This says that you are paying attention. This may sound ridiculously paranoid if you are reading this in a place where theft is not such a big problem. I assure you, when you get to the crowded markets in Peru, you will see plenty of people with their backpacks on the front.

When you go to exit any vehicle–bus, taxi, collectivo or airplane, do not allow yourself to be rushed out. Always look behind you and underneath your seat to see if you left anything behind. If you leave it behind, you will never see it again.

Be prepared with what you need in hand so that you are not fumbling around and feeling rushed. You are very vulnerable when you are in that state.

You are also very vulnerable when you are paying for something and your wallet is out, though perhaps not for the reason you might think. You are so focused on counting your money and paying that you don't notice that someone is helping themselves to your pockets or backpack.

If anyone touches you at all, be alert! Thieves work together and will use distraction to make you vulnerable. One will spill something on you, perhaps even apologizing and offering to help you clean up the mess with profuse apologies. In the meantime, while you are in the resulting state of shock and distracted, another one or two will sideswipe you and your pockets will be emptied or your bag will be slit. Their timing will be so perfect that you won't even notice their act.

This happened to one of my friends. One person was upstairs hanging out the window and when she was targeted, he dropped confetti on her head. There were two accomplices on the street, and at the precise moment the confetti landed on her head, she looked up and was side-swiped on both sides, leaving pockets empty.

Here are some other guidelines:

- Do not be flashy with what you have; e.g., money, jewelry, cameras, etc.

- Do not travel alone through isolated areas, even in daylight.

- Always take a taxi at night after 9:00 p.m.

- Never leave your belongings without a trusted guard, not even for five seconds

- If possible, wear your purse on the inside of your jacket.

- If you are on the street carrying a shoulder bag, wear it on the building side, not the street side. People drive by in vehicles and snatch it off your shoulder and are gone before you can react.

- Do not wander the streets inebriated. There is a whole underbelly of thieves who prey on drunken tourists.

Never leave your drink in a bar to go dancing. I have spoken to many people who have absolutely no idea what happened because, while they weren't looking, someone slipped a drug into their drink (usually roofies). They wake up the next morning in a strange place, robbed and sometimes raped.

DOGS

There are lots and lots of dogs in Peru. Tourists are always taken aback by the dogs. They are everywhere. You can be out in the back of beyond, miles away from anything resembling civilization, and a dog will find you.

Peruvian dogs are nothing like Western dogs in their behavior. Of course, in their natural environment, dogs are pack animals and social creatures. In the West, we have replaced the pack with ourselves, and our animals look to us to meet all their social needs. Many of them are neurotic as a result of not having enough (or sometimes too much) attention to adequately meet their social needs.

Peruvian dogs are free of this, for the most part. They are usually outdoors and have their own territory and social hierarchy with other dogs. If you expect to stop a street dog for attention when he is "doing his rounds," he will likely look at you like "Excuse me! I have places to go and things to do!" They do not need people socially so much. There are territories to mark, butts to sniff, and as they make their rounds, it is the doggie version of reading the news or checking Facebook.

You won't see many cats in town. They are all hiding or living up on the rooftops. Peru is not a safe place for cats.

And it all happens in the street. No child here ever wonders how puppies are made. When a female is in heat, there is a pack of dogs surrounding her. I have seen as many as 15 dogs vying for position in the mating hierarchy and there is plenty of barking and fighting, and there is NO chance she is not going to get pregnant.

Street animals are rarely spayed or neutered and rarely vaccinated against diseases in Peru. Consequently, their lives are short relative to the dogs in first world countries. But they seem to be happy in their short lives, being DOGS instead of some of the bizarre, neurotic beings that you find on the end of leash or tucked under someone's arm in the U.S.

There are so many dogs in my neighborhood that some people won't consider living in the area. They can be very territorial as they guard the area surrounding their house. Since my neighborhood has no vehicular traffic, I think there are more dogs than usual, and with the lack of public traffic the dogs are more territorial than usual for their tiny urban patch of grass and concrete. I have been grateful on more than one occasion to have had a backpack with me that I could put between me and a territorial dog.

Whenever I have commented to the residents how many dogs there are, they always respond, "Well, it is either the dogs or thieves–take your pick!"

There are two ways of dealing with the dogs. One is to carry rocks with you. Dogs really don't like it when you throw rocks at them and they take off running even when you raise your arm like you are about to throw one. That one took a little while for me to figure out. I would go to toss a piece of what I was eating their way, to share with them, and they would always run away. Later it became apparent why.

The other way of dealing with them is to always take the same route so that the dogs you are passing en route know you. Once they know you it isn't a problem.

Part 3

My New World

A Symphony of Sounds in My New World

It is a Sunday morning in July, which is winter in the Southern Hemisphere, and I am lying on the sofa in my apartment in Cusco. I have spent the morning drinking cups of tea, eating, reading and trying to stay warm. My feet stay cold this morning and I don't know why. I have two heaters going in this room, I am sitting on my sofa under a down comforter and I am wearing warm socks. Still my feet are cold. I remove my socks and take turns tucking my cold feet in the crook of the knee of the other leg. Eventually that works. I think to myself, *I really need to get a hot water bottle.*

There are so many sounds I can hear, and each one has a story to tell.

This is what I hear: a constant symphony of the chirping of sparrows in the background, the hum of my refrigerator, the constant ticking of one of my oil-filled radiators which appears to have an air bubble, and the various barks, yaps and yelps of the neighborhood dogs.

Firecrackers go off nearby. This happens a lot. I have heard several stories of why this is. One is that it is to scare off evil spirits, but the boys that I have seen setting them off don't look very frightened to me. Each day is assigned a certain saint, and is known as that particular "Saint's Day" and the fireworks are also to celebrate the saints.

Another story that I read said that this started when the Spanish first came in the 1500's. The Inka had never heard cannons before and they thought that the Spanish had harnessed the power of thunder, and this desire for all the "boom-boom" is leftover from that time. I personally think that they just like to make a lot of noise, like boys do. I do wish they wouldn't start so early in the morning though!

A car honks its horn on the road above my apartment. I can hear men yelling in the distance, like they do at a football game. Someone is whistling. It is consistent enough that I suspect that it is either birds or some kind of recording. I can hear a bird singing, that one is a real bird.

The neighbors are out doing their Sunday morning things and making all kinds of interesting noises. Out of curiosity, I have to get up off the sofa to see what the heck they are doing. One man is hitting the side of his building with a crowbar and knocking off the stucco, the sound of the metal clanking on concrete reverberates in my head. I wonder why he is doing that. Now he is sweeping the exposed concrete underneath the stucco. *What is the point*, I wonder? Now he is throwing buckets of water at the wall. Fascinating… People fascinate me.

Another neighbor and his two children are in their fenced in and overgrown garden patch. The man is moving trash from one side to the other and the boys have hedge clippers and some metal tool and are whacking away at a rose bush hedge. The man's pants keep falling down, exposing the crack of his ass and he keeps hitching them up.

The sun is shining on the high mountains of the Andes in the distance. Now I am going back to the sofa to see if my warm spot it still there.

A car siren goes off—the type that changes tone every couple of seconds. This is one of the more annoying sounds in Cusco. These sirens go off so frequently that no one even pays any attention to them. I can hear my landlady's cell phone going off in the apartment downstairs. That has got to be one of the most obnoxious cell phone rings on the planet. It frequently starts as soon as 6AM.

I hear someone slam the metal entry door to our apartment building with a huge "clang!" and I hear the voices of children. My landlady's "*nietos negritos*" (little black grandchildren), as she calls them, are running up the stairs, laughing and shouting. They aren't really black, they are just not exactly white. They call them *moreno* (brown) in Peru. The Peruvians do not bother with the political correctness of words. If you are skinny they call you "Skinny" (*Flaca*), if you are chubby they call you "Chubby" (*Gordito*), and they do it with affection.

Beep-beep–the friendly honking of a passing car that is announcing that he is where he is. There is the sound of a car with a muffler that is not working well in the distance. Ah, there is the sound of the whistle of our passing neighborhood security guard saying "I am here!"

From my sofa I can see someone on the roof of the building across from ours hanging up her laundry–whites today. From my living room window I can frequently see her little boys, the ones that are currently in the garden with their father, jumping on the sofa wearing just their underwear while watching TV.

They have a pet beagle that lives on the rooftop. Poor little guy never gets to go out of that building and I feel for him. Sometimes he spends the whole afternoon jumping up and down to peer over the wall, just for a view of something besides concrete. I see his little head appear briefly above the wall, his ears flapping with each jump. I stand up on the rooftop terrace of my building as I hang up my laundry and look down to him and send him some love.

Now I hear the distinct scraping sound of the stuccoing of a wall. Must be my neighbor.

I hear more barking. The dog sounds here really dominate. Heaven forbid when someone is in heat! There was so much barking going on that one of my roommates, when she first moved in, called out from her bed, "What the heck is going on out there?!"

A rooster crows. I hear that guy all the time, but I have never seen him. In trying to locate from whence the sound comes, I think it is from an unfinished apartment building nearby. Cracks me up. You would never hear this sound in suburban America.

Chickens are very much a part of life in Peru, not just a grocery store item you see wrapped up in plastic in the meat department at your local supermarket. I was with a girlfriend the other day on a local bus in the Sacred Valley. An old *campesina* woman with long, gray braided pigtails called out "*Baja!*" (Down!), meaning that she wanted off at the next bus stop. She had left a large bag at the door of the van when she went to take her seat. My girlfriend, with the best of intentions, went to help her with her bag of what she assumed were heavy potatoes. Much to her surprise, the contents of the bag started flapping about, causing quite a stir and the chickens inside managed to peck her a couple of times through the bag. She shrieked and the entire bus erupted in laughter!

More sounds…I hear the putt-putt of a motorcycle. They drive through the neighborhood sidewalks delivering canisters of bottled gas. There is the sound of a vehicle straining in a lower gear to get up the hill.

I hear more hammering-like sounds …gotta get up and look. It is the gardening neighbor slamming a hoe into the hard soil of his garden. His wife comes out of the house wearing yellow rubber kitchen gloves, calling him: "Nano! Nano! Nano!"

Ok, now I go back to the sofa. One neighbor now has his TV on very loud and it adds to the background drone of sounds. I hear more hammering, and perhaps someone with a pick. *What the heck are they doing?* Leaving my warm spot on the sofa is difficult, but once again, my curiosity gets the better of me.

Oh, now the constructing neighbor is throwing handfuls of concrete at the place where he knocked off the stucco. The gardening neighbor, Nano, is dragging a small dead tree INTO his gardening patch and sharing a smile and word with the constructing neighbor.

A fly is buzzing in my window. I open the window to usher him out, and another, bigger one flies in. Great… there is an infinity of flies near the garbage dumping area. My sofa beckons once again.

Someone has their truck in reverse and it is making the loud, distinct "I am backing up" warning beeps.

A suspicious snapping sound has me heading back to the window. I abandon the idea of staying in my warm spot on the sofa and surrender to just taking the comforter with me to the window and wrapping it around me.

Nano is sitting on the ground in his garden and he has a small mound of rocks from which smoke is billowing. He is snapping the dead tree into small sticks and feeding the fire. Nice. Ah, I see, they are roasting potatoes in that little oven they have made. This time of year in Cusco this is common practice, they call it *watia*. This is a tradition they have done in Peru for thousands of years, potatoes baked in an earthen oven.

One of the boys has come out and now they are eyeing and kicking the broken-down gate to their garden. One son leaves and comes back with a hammer. Hmmmm.....I thought they were going to fix the gate but it looks like its fate is the fire.

Many dogs are barking now—dog fight!

There is a proper, paved road above the dirt road behind my neighborhood. Because of the incline of the hill, this paved road is about 20 feet higher than the dirt road. A stone wall has been built with a supporting terrace and a row of trees has been planted in the terrace between the two roads. There is a smallish group of people parading down this street now, carrying the effigy of a saint. A brass band follows them, playing festively. Peru is definitely the place to be if you want to be in a brass band! There are many opportunities to play. Recently, I ran out of my apartment and down the sidewalk to take photos of a procession I could hear that had a brass band playing, only to find upon my arrival that they were unloading a casket from a vehicle. I guess they play at funerals as well.

The Peruvians are very festive people. They don't need much of an excuse to celebrate. Their parties go on for much longer than I can. Inti Raymi, their Winter Solstice in June, goes on for more than three weeks!

I read the chronicles that were written by the first literate people in Cusco in the 1500s only to learn that this is an Inkan tradition, this constant celebration. It has been going on for hundreds, if not thousands of years. They believe that Pachamama (Mother Earth) *wants* us to be happy and it is a gift we give her to share our joy! I love this!!

Their ongoing festivity makes me very happy! There are ornate costumes and twirling old ladies with their bowler hats and fringed shawls and men with masks that border on the obscene, with noses that look downright phallic in nature. These are the *Majeños* and are meant to poke fun at the traffickers of wine and spirits in the old colony who imported alcohol from the Majes River Valley near Arequipa in the south, by mule trains across the high Andes. Their costumes are always pot-bellied, with leather jackets, riding breeches, boots with spurs and a bottle of beer in one hand, staggering around as if they are drunk. One time I was walking home through my neighborhood and all the traffic had been stopped (which is not an unusual occurrence in Cusco) and they were all dancing in the street, staggering around as if drunk (which perhaps they were!). One of the young men was lying down on his back in the middle of the road and wearing two of these masks with the long phallic noses–one on his face, and the other on his crotch!

There are sometimes young men stomping their feet as they dance, with gigantic bells in every color (we would call them jingle-bells, they call them *cascabeles*) sewn into the legs of their pants. Even when they are not dancing and just walking down the street they make a wonderful jingling sound. There are beautiful young women in short skirts and high-heels showing off their pretty brown legs, who have long black braided extensions and ribbons woven into their pigtails and, of course, there is always the ever-present brass band.

I don't think you need a permit to close a road in Cusco for a festival, they happen most days!

****

I love my neighborhood in Cusco. It is a pedestrian-only neighborhood with no access for vehicular traffic. Therefore, it does not have the constant beeping of car horns or billows of exhaust fumes. It is 4 or 5 blocks long by 4 or 5 blocks deep. It is called *Zaguan del Cielo*, which means something like "Passageway to Heaven." That might be a slight over-statement, but I'm good with that.

It is very urban-suburban, if that makes sense. It is within walking distance of the town center, though not a tourist area. There are lots of families and a pretty stable population, unlike other areas that can have a high turnover and be transient with the very mobile population of Cusco. My neighborhood is very Peruvian middle class. But it is nothing like the peace and quiet of an average suburb in the U.S.A.

I love the symphony of sounds in my neighborhood. Various vendors come through with their wares in the mornings. As they come through the neighborhood, each has a distinct sound that they make, to let the residents know that they are there. There is the guy with a huge basket of bread on his back who honks a duck horn. There is a guy with a wheeled and foot-pedal driven knife sharpener and he blows a multi-toned whistle. People come through selling fruit or looking to buy scrap metal and broken machines, calling out as they pass through.

There is the sound of parents who are accompanying their little children, dressed in their cute uniforms off to school, hurrying them along. There is the sound of the slapping of little shoes on the concrete sidewalks that make up this residential labyrinth, with the parents calling out an occasional "*Apurate!*" (Hurry up!)

There is a neighbor who is constantly losing his well-groomed terrier calling "*Yaku! Yaku!*" (Jacob!) This has actually gotten to be laughable because it is so predictable. Yaku never comes until he is ready!

One of my absolute favorite sounds happens Mondays, Wednesdays and Fridays around 5:00pm. A person runs through the neighborhood clanging a cow bell. All of the residents react with a Pavlovian response and run for their trash cans. The cowbell clanging means that the garbage truck will be there within 10 or 15 minutes. At the top of the neighborhood, which is on an incline of one of the many hills in Cusco, there is a dirt road which gives vehicular access to those of us who live at the top. Everyone comes running out of their houses with their little bags of trash. They heap it all right next to the sign that says in big red letters *Prohibido Botar Basura* (Prohibited to Throw Trash) then says in much smaller letters beneath "except Mon-Wed-Fri at 5:00." Recycling has been slow to come to Cusco in an organized way, so there are people that take that 15 minute window to come over and sort through the trash to collect recyclable plastics and glass to turn in for cash. The garbage truck then comes down this dirt road (which turns into a mud pit during rainy season) and the garbage guys then actually go through the trash and pull out any remaining recyclables.

The trash is not put out in advance because of the dogs. During that 15 minute window, the dogs all know that there is a veritable feast in there for them. They come over and when they catch a whiff of something that they may find tasty, they take the whole bag off to a corner somewhere and devour the contents with no regard whatsoever for the trash-strewn mess that they have left behind.

One of my least favorite sounds is the security guard who patrols the neighborhood. He blows a very shrill police whistle every fifteen seconds. I suspect that the reason he blows the whistle is to let the paying residents know that he is there doing his job. It also occurs to me that a security guard may want to keep a lower profile if he actually wants to catch any potential thieves. Instead, this whistle just lets the thieves know where he is, so they go somewhere else. This shrill whistling goes on all night as he makes his rounds and it constantly jolted me out of my slumber when I first moved there, until I finally located ear plugs. Ear plugs are essential if you are not a heavy sleeper! I have this ongoing vision in my mind of what I would like to do with that whistle when it jars me from my sleep in the middle of the night…

There is an orange cat who meows incessantly, just wandering the neighborhood. How he gets away with it I do not know. Cusco is not really a safe place for cats since there are so many dogs running free.

****

If you are looking for total peace and quiet where you live, Peru should probably not be your top choice...

Tantra - A New Chapter in My Life

It had been about six years since my husband and I had separated. I had started referring to him as my "was-bund." We still had not divorced so he wasn't really my ex-husband, but he was most definitely no longer a husband to me. For the first few years of our separation, I had absolutely no interest in pursuing a relationship with another man. That last one had taken so much out of me.

During the difficult years of our marriage, I had gained 30 pounds while using food to try to fill the emptiness I was feeling. I did not feel physically attractive. While still in the U.S., one day I decided that I just was not happy with my body, and I decided to go ahead and lose the 30 pounds. It took me about six months. I was surprised to find how much better I felt. Suddenly, I had begun to attract the attention of men again. This completely freaked me out. It had been so long since I had dated, about 25 years, I really had no idea how to handle it.

There was a big problem though–every man that I attracted and was attracted to was an alcoholic to some degree. There had been a problem with alcoholism in my family my entire life. It was very familiar to me, and it wasn't until after my husband and I split up that I even realized it was a problem. Once I finally educated myself about alcoholism, I learned that it had been one of the key problems in our marriage. I had come to the conclusion that it wasn't possible to have a truly intimate relationship when alcohol was involved to the level that it had been in our marriage. I had decided that if I was ever going to have a healthy, deeply intimate relationship with a man, that he could not be an active alcoholic.

In the month after I lost the weight and started feeling better about myself and dressing differently, I had four different men express an interest in having a relationship with me. They were all alcoholics.

I clearly had more work to do if I was going to change who I was attracting. I made a conscious effort in doing this, and it was taking years. Still, every man I attracted had a drinking problem. However, I was determined to change this aspect of my life.

I was really missing having the opportunity to express myself sexually. Sexual expression had always been very much a part of my being, and I was really missing it. About four years after our separation, I had attempted to start a relationship with a man, but it quickly became apparent to me that I really wasn't ready yet. My thinking was still falling into the old, familiar patterns (he should do this, he should do that, he should call me–"shoulding" all over the place! Not exactly the non-judgmental, unconditional love I was striving for). At least I was now recognizing them and not projecting them onto him, but they were driving me nuts. I needed more time.

I had always been intrigued by the concept of Tantric sex. Tantra is a branch of an Asian system of beliefs and practices. Tantric sex is one aspect that holds that sexual experiences can be sacred acts which are capable of elevating their participants to a higher spiritual plane, which I saw as using the sexual energy of an intimate relationship to enhance one's spiritual life. The key problem was that I didn't have a partner. I had met a man who wrote a book that claimed you could transform your life by using the power of the energies created by using sacred sexuality. He claimed that you didn't necessarily need a partner to practice Tantric sex. This was good news for me!

I had been practicing the exercises in his book for about a year. I had gotten to the point where I knew how to use the powerful creative force of sexual energy to enhance my own health and well-being. I felt that I had gotten back in touch with my own sexual energies, and I had gotten as far as I could with using Tantra alone. I was hoping to be able to attract a partner who also had an interest in this form of sacred sexuality with whom I could explore the next level–working with a partner.

As appealing as this was to me, the concept was also very frightening. I had absolutely no idea what my body was capable of or how it would react during love-making. Since I had been sexually active, I had been through a thyroidectomy and menopause, both of which had profound effects on my body and how it functioned.

How would my heart handle it? My heart had been shattered into a million little pieces which I thought would never come back together again.

This was clearly going to take a lot of courage.

In the past, people had frequently referred to me as brave for having done some of the things I had done. I used to correct them and say, "No, I can't really claim to be brave. To be brave you have to overcome fear, and the truth of the matter is that I didn't have a lot of fear. A better word would be fearless. I have been fairly fearless."

Somehow, having babies changed that for me. Being responsible for myself was one thing. Feeling responsible for somebody else when I frequently didn't have control over their actions and best interests had turned me into a very anxious person.

I was determined to overcome the anxiety and attract more healthy men!

Vibeing in Angelo

Ingrid and I had gone up the mountain to Tambillo to attend Kush and Erica's wedding at their house. Silly us, we arrived at the time we were told to be there, and they were not even dressed yet. I should have known by then that what we consider "on time" is way too early for Peruvians. We were told to come back in an hour, so we went to go visit a friend that lived nearby. When we rang the doorbell to his walled compound, a man answered the door and told us that our friend was not in. He briefly introduced himself to us as Angelo, from the U.S., and then excused himself since he was in the process of painting as evidenced by the paint spatters all over him.

Ingrid and I had been in Peru for about six months and I was focused on my work, improving my Spanish and learning about Peruvian culture. Even though I spent less than one minute talking to Angelo, I got an immediate "hit" that he was a potential candidate for a relationship with me. I intended to pursue this, as it was rare for me to feel such an attraction!

My plan was for Ingrid and me to invite our friend and Angelo over to dinner one night to get the opportunity to know Angelo better and explore the possibility of him and me getting together.

Shortly thereafter, I ran into the friend that Angelo was living with and I got his phone number so that we could arrange for us all to get together for dinner. The phone number was written on a tiny scrap of paper, the corner of a page that had been ripped off of something, and it had their names and phone number on it. It was sitting on a table in our apartment.

The next week our lives went absolutely crazy. A key employee at the hotel, who I had become very good friends with, died unexpectedly. One day he and I had spent the entire day making a plan for work for the next year, and the next day we were at his funeral. That was quite a shock to me, and we felt very sad.

Then Ingrid and I had to go to Lima to finalize our work permits for Peru. We found ourselves in Lima for almost a week. When we returned Ingrid found out that her father was very ill and she had to take a leave of absence from work to go to Germany to see him.

So I was living in the apartment alone and reeling a bit from all of the recent events. I didn't really feel comfortable inviting both guys over to dinner while I was there alone. The little scrap of paper with the names and phone number on it just sat on the table in my apartment. Every day I would pass it by two or three times and say to myself, "How am I going to finagle meeting up with Angelo?"

In my meditations in the mornings I always ask for guidance and help in accomplishing things that would be good for my soul's path. I had been practicing using my energy and intention to make myself a magnet for people and experiences that would enhance my life. I had a couple of very unusual and synchronistic things that had happened that I saw as evidence that this was working.

As an example, one morning there was a lady who was having breakfast at the restaurant in the hotel. It was quite unusual for people to come in from the street for breakfast. She struck me as a very interesting person and since I was the Guest Relations Manager of the hotel I had every excuse to approach her and start a conversation. She said she had absolutely no idea why, but as she was passing the hotel (which looks very nondescript from the outside) she was compelled to come in. We became very good friends and I learned that she was also very attuned to using her own intuition and listening to the "nudges" and guidance that she received.

A most amazing thing happened one morning shortly thereafter. Over the next few days, I kept walking past that little scrap of paper with the names and phone number that was sitting on the table in my apartment for days, wondering how I was going to connect with Angelo.

Usually when I was at work I was tucked away in some part of the hotel at the back, but for some reason I was headed for Reception at the front of the hotel. I looked up, and Angelo was walking into the lobby! I could not believe my eyes!

"Angelo! What in the world are you doing here?!" I exclaimed. He had no idea who I was, he didn't remember meeting me. It had been a month ago, the meeting had been less than a minute, and at the time he was obviously preoccupied with painting. He looked around himself to see if perhaps I was talking to somebody else, looking quite baffled.

I said, "You are Angelo, aren't you?"

He said, "Well ... yes ... but am I the right Angelo?"

"Yes, indeed, I think you are!" I said. I proceeded to remind him of the occasion of our meeting. Then I offered to give him a tour of our beautiful boutique hotel and invited him to have a cup of tea with me. I couldn't believe my luck. He explained that he had never been in this hotel before but that he was looking for a friend that he thought might be there. His friend wasn't there. We had a lovely chat and I definitely felt that there was good potential for us to meet again and that there was a mutual attraction.

The next week was Thanksgiving. Ingrid was still gone and it was my first Thanksgiving in Peru. I was feeling a bit blue since Thanksgiving is one of my favorite holidays and I had no one to celebrate it with. I checked around and I couldn't find any place in Cusco that was even acknowledging Thanksgiving. I decided to call Angelo and ask him if he knew of a place where I might find Thanksgiving dinner.

"Sure!" he said, "I am cooking and you can come celebrate Thanksgiving with me."

Dinner was lovely, though it was not at all what I was expecting. Angelo had cooked roasted alpaca and *papas a la huancaina*–potatoes with a sauce made from the Peruvian pepper, *aji* and peanuts, amongst other things. Peruvian Thanksgiving!

We got to know each other a bit better and we set a date to meet for lunch at a local pizza place the next day.

****

The next day, I was so nervous! How was I going to do this??

So I just blurted it out, "I have been studying Tantric sex lately. Are you familiar with it?"

He was vaguely familiar with it.

"I have been working with it for a while, and I feel that I am ready to take the next step, to go deeper into it. I am looking for a partner and I am very attracted to you. Are you in a relationship with anyone now?"

I think his jaw hit the floor.

"Um…uh…yes…I mean…no. Well, I mean…um, I'm actually having a relationship with myself," he said. He then went on to explain that he'd been doing a lot of "spiritual work," so he had been focusing his energies on that.

"Would you be interested in having a relationship with me?"

"Uh, yes! I think I could do that!"

Wooo-hooo and yippie! Thaaank you!

****

Angelo and I started seeing each other. He was super sweet and I learned that he was really quite a phenomenal man. Naturally, he was an alcoholic, but he had come to Peru to use the plant medicines available and legal in Peru to heal his alcoholism.

Alcoholism had been rife in his family and he had lost many family members as a result of it. He had failed marriages, trouble with the law, and in spite of trying everything he possibly could, he had not been able to stop drinking. He had come to Peru a few months earlier and had gone into the jungle to see if Ayahuasca could help him. The spirit of Ayahuasca had told him, "I am not your medicine. Go to a place in the clouds and experience San Pedro."

Angelo had come to Cusco to work with San Pedro to cure his alcoholism. When I had first met him a month earlier he was still drinking. He told me of an experience he had while under the influence of San Pedro. He said that he felt such a rage at the control that alcohol had in his life and his inability to resist it. He was at the house where he was staying when this rage came over him. There was a bottle of vodka in the house. In his fury he went into the house and got the bottle of vodka and came out into the garden and smashed the bottle of vodka on a rock. He said that in his altered state he saw all of the little pieces of broken glass sprout pink wings and fly away. As he watched them fly away he called out, "Now set my Spirit free!"

He has not had a drink since.

All that time I was wondering why I couldn't seem to get together with Angelo. I choose to believe that I get what I ask for in my meditations and it seemed to me that the reason I was not finding the opportunity to get together with Angelo was because it just wasn't the right time yet. He had to go through his processes to get where he was and to become the man I was looking for.

The relationship was extremely healing for me. Angelo was an alcoholic but he was no longer an active alcoholic. We both agreed that alcohol would not be a part of our relationship together. This had implications that I really was not expecting. Not only had it been years since I'd had an intimate relationship, I realized that in most cases I had been in the habit of having a drink or two before having sex for most of my life. I had always used wine or a cocktail or two to help me relax. Of course, this has a numbing effect which can be quite pleasurable, but it also numbs consciousness.

In my relationship with Angelo I had to show up and be fully present and fully conscious. It was terrifying to begin with! Deep intimacy can be quite frightening. We moved through this and it took me to a new level, which was exactly what I had been wanting.

Our intimate relationship lasted for a few months. I have heard it said that people come into our lives for "a reason, a season, or a lifetime," depending on what it is our soul needs to accomplish with that person.

One day Angelo and I looked at each other and realized that we had accomplished what we had come together to accomplish, and it was time for us to redefine our relationship. There is a great strength in acknowledging when it is time to move on in a relationship, and not being attached to what you thought it was or what you thought it was going to be. I learned that lesson the hard way when it took me so many years to accept that my marriage was not going to be forever, despite our best laid plans. I suffered so much because what "was" was not what I thought it was going to be. One day I learned that my happiness was in my own hands. All I had to do was learn to "love what is," and let go of what used to be.

Angelo had lived up to his name–he was indeed an angel for me. He helped me take my sexual energy to a new level with consciousness and learn more about what my body and I were capable of in working with a partner in Tantric sex.

I saw Angelo first and foremost as an incredibly courageous man. When one has been an alcoholic for so many years, much damage has usually been done in past relationships. To be willing to go back and face that and rectify the damage done takes immense strength and humility.

Tantric sex requires a level of intimacy that scares most men off. Angelo was willing to walk this path with me for a while. When one is making love to the divinity in another person, it is at once more impersonal and simultaneously deeply intimate. It certainly takes courage.

Angelo and I have remained dear friends. He did heal himself with San Pedro. He stopped drinking and a few years later married a Peruvian woman.

I was so grateful to have the opportunity to have a relationship with him. I would've never imagined that this would be how I would heal my own issues with alcoholism and men in my life.

It has been years since that happened, and I'm happy to say that I have finally broken that tendency to attract and be attracted to alcoholic men.

Peruvian Men

Peruvian men can be some of the sweetest people on the planet.

Having a relationship with a Peruvian man can also be extremely challenging for someone from a Western culture. I speak not only from my own experience but from many, many, many conversations with my girlfriends over the years.

If you ask around, you will find that the men from different parts of Peru have different reputations. The ones from Lima and Arequipa have a reputation for being more like Western men, more sophisticated and better educated, with a lot of Spanish ancestry and frequently fairer skin. The Cusqueñeans tend to be more reserved in their expression of emotion. This is a survival trait learned from hundreds of years of oppression by the Spanish and the Inka Empire, but they are very deeply emotional. The Cusqueñeans usually have more indigenous ancestry, shorter stature, darker skin, and barrel-shaped chests to accommodate larger lungs from generations of high-altitude living. Just like in many countries, the big city people tend to look down on the people from the country and mountains. They consider them to be slow-thinking, resistant to change, and hard-headed. The men from northern Peru have a reputation for being the sweetest.

For reasons which I have not fully understood, many Peruvian men find gringa women very attractive. So, while in the United States I was rarely noticed by the self-absorbed, detached tendencies of the men, suddenly I found myself in a place where I was considered to be attractive and desirable. I was gushing to a good friend about what a surprise this was. How delightful it was to be seen as attractive after many years of feeling quite average. She had lived there for several years longer than I and seemed to have the Peruvian psyche nailed. She put it quite succinctly when she said to me, "Don't take it personally, Lisa, they'll fuck anyone."

126

Though it may sound a bit harsh, it actually helped me to put things into perspective, because unfortunately, it is frequently quite true. The general consensus amongst the people I spoke with is that they have a much higher libido than Western men. And, be warned: Peruvian men are quite fertile.

I started to see a pattern of 30-something year old gringa women becoming pregnant by Peruvian men. So I did a little informal count, and I counted 20 women that I knew in a two year period who had unplanned pregnancies. In most cases, the man was not interested in taking responsibility for a child. The ones that were initially willing to step up to the plate tended to lose interest after a short while.

Don't get me wrong, I'm not saying the Peruvians are not good fathers. The family status is held in extremely high regard in Peru. I saw many men dote on their children and shower them with affection. What I am saying is this: from what I saw, if having the "family status" with a Peruvian man was not the basis of your relationship with him, he's most likely not going to stick around if you get pregnant.

I even suspect that some of these women who find themselves near the end of their child-bearing years are taking advantage of the opportunity to have a child without the constraints of marriage that this situation offers. A very interesting phenomenon, indeed.

****

I had been living in Cusco for a year and a half before I first stuck my toe in the water of learning the ways of Peruvian men. The first year in Cusco I was more focused on my work, learning the language, trying to understand the culture and learning how to navigate my way through this new life I was creating for myself. I felt I had successfully re-entered the world of intimate relationships with men again with Angelo, and I thought I would like to give it another try. Peruvian men were abundant, and many of them seemed to be attracted to me. So I thought it was time to give it a shot!

It was my birthday, and my goal was to learn a little bit about the nightlife. I invited four of my girlfriends who already knew Cusco by Night to go out on the town with me and show me the ropes. First we went out for pizza, and then we did a sampling of a few of the many nightlife options in central Cusco.

The places we went to that night were all within three or four blocks of each other. We went into different kinds of places, some with live music, some discos, some with salsa and some others. We had a great time, and I was reminded that there is an entirely different world at night in Cusco! In previous years in Cusco, I had gone out a few times at night. But during this period, I had to be at work early, and since things don't really get started until about 11 p.m. in Cusco, the nightlife had not really been an option for me.

It was probably about 1:00 in the morning, and we were pretty well oiled by that time. We were at a salsa club, and I was sitting near the dance floor watching the dancers. Salsa is really not my rhythm and, despite several lessons, I had not been able to get it. A man came over and asked me to dance. I thanked him for the invitation but told him I didn't know how to dance salsa, to which he replied, "Neither do I." It seemed to me like a pretty generous admission and since I wasn't really at risk of embarrassing myself I thought, "Well, what the heck?" and I danced with him. I hadn't been out dancing in a very long time, and it was nice, even though this man didn't look like anyone I thought I would ever be attracted to, and he was perhaps a little young for me. As we danced, he held my hand and put his other arm around my waist. We were cheek to cheek. I liked the way he felt and smelled. This kind of surprised me…

I must have told him that it was time for me to go home, and he asked me if he could walk me home.

"You can walk me home, but you can't come in." I told him.

"I didn't ask to come in, I asked if I can walk you home. It is late."

Fair enough. Okay, why not?

He walked me home. He was very gentlemanly, and when we got to my door he asked me if he could take me out the next day to buy me a cake for my birthday. I thought that was very sweet, even though I'm really not that crazy about birthday cake. It did kind of catch me off guard, so I agreed to it. The next morning I thought, "This guy isn't even really my type, and yet I agreed to meet him again, so I have to do it. What can I do to put him off? I know what: I'll wear my glasses and no makeup. That should do it."

I met him, and we hopped in a taxi and went to a bakery where he bought me a whole birthday cake. He was very polite and seemed very interested in me in spite of the fact that I was doing absolutely nothing to try to make myself more appealing or attractive. I found this a bit novel.

I said to him, "I'm a bit older than you."

To which he replied, "I like that."

I thought, "Well, I haven't dated anybody in a while. This guy seems to like me. He seems nice enough. I have nothing to lose. I'll go out with him a couple of times and see what happens. Maybe get back in practice."

He was a trekking guide and in excellent physical shape. His upper arms were like hams, massive and strong and I found them sexy. He was of Quechua descent with the typical barrel chest, mocha-colored skin, jet black hair and, well… he was Catholic. I couldn't believe I was actually seeing him. I typically go for much more sensitive men, and he was very clearly a man's man. I even had to take out my contact lenses for the first few times to get used to what he looked like, he was SO "not my type!" (OK, trying to be open-minded here and getting over physical appearances….) I found it quite surprising that he was okay with the age difference. I called him Pumita, Little Puma. In the Andean culture the puma is the symbol of the Kaypacha–the physical world in which we live.

There were a few really sweet things about him. He was considered to be *serrano* and he took great pride and felt great love for the mountains. The Peruvian culture puts a very high value on marital and family status. When asked why he wasn't married, as people frequently do ask, he would say, "I am married to the mountains."

One time as he was leaving my apartment, there was a terrible storm, and it was pouring rain. As I saw him off at the front door, I told him that I felt bad sending him out in this terrible weather. He said, "Don't worry about me, I am a Man of the Mountains." Very sweet.

Pumita is also responsible for what I consider to be the very best example of bizarre excuses as to why the Peruvians frequently don't do what they say they'll do.

We had agreed to meet in Plaza Regocijo at 5:00 after I got off work. It was raining so I took my raincoat and umbrella and walked over to Plaza Regocijo. I waited for him for half an hour. He never showed up. I spoke to him the next day on the telephone and I asked him why he never showed up? His response was this:

"I had to take my mother down into the Sacred Valley. I would have called you, but it was raining."

This bizarre excuse was a foreshadowing of what came to be a cause of much frustration in my life over the next years.

Pumita and I went out for a few months, and it was an emotional roller coaster ride for me. It was my introduction into the machisto dating world. I was so frequently offended by his machismo behaviors that I was sending him off packing on a regular basis. I remember one time I told him that I was so annoyed with him that I needed for him to just not contact me for a week, to give me time to settle down and see if I could have a coherent thought. His response was to try to call me, text me, and stop by my apartment until I finally told him, "Now we have two problems–what you did, and now how you are handling it. You are not honoring my request for space." He liked the drama. I did not.

He was starting up a new business and he felt very strongly that I should be willing to work with him. I already had a job, and I told him, "We are not even on speaking terms at least half of the time. The last thing in the world I want to do is work with you."

To which he replied, "If you love me, you will work with me." This resulted in another attempt by me to end our relationship. But he was very persistent.

I found that due to the difference in our ages, we were in very different stages in life. He was very ambitious and gung ho about his new business venture, and he wanted me to share in his enthusiasm. I had already accomplished the things I wanted to accomplish in the business world, and I was just looking to have a more peaceful time and enjoy my life after all my hard work of the past.

One day we were having a discussion about the level of drama that I felt he needed in our relationship, which I understand is not uncommon in many Latin cultures.

He looked at me and in all seriousness and sincerity said to me, "Do you need to suffer?"

"Absolutely not," was my response.

"Well, some people do," he replied, very matter-of-factly. At this point, I got the message that I was dealing with a very deep-seated core belief, probably stemming from the fact that he was Catholic and Latin. I decided that I'd had enough. That was the end of that relationship.

****

I did have one other very near miss with a Cusqueñean man that pretty well sealed my decision that they were not for me. This one seemed like a lovely man in many, many ways. He was also in tourism, and I had worked with him on many different occasions, and we'd gotten to be good friends. I'd known him for about four months when it became apparent that there was a smoldering attraction between us. We had been out in the Sacred Valley for the day and were in very close proximity to each other on the drive back to Cusco, which had been painful for us both due to the unexpressed attraction.

We were crammed together in the cab of a tiny truck that he had borrowed for the trip and we had been sharing some deeply personal conversations about our lives in the hours that it took to return to Cusco. He asked me if he could hold my hand. The energetic exchange between us was absolutely electrifying.

I found it somewhat amusing that the car kept overheating on our trip back. We had to keep pulling over to the side of the road, get out of the cab, and pull the seats forward to access the engine which was located under panels beneath our seats. He had several bottles of water with him which he would then pour over the engine to cool it down. Steam would billow up, and the whole thing seemed an accurate representation of what was going on between us energetically. There were a couple of girlfriends who had joined us on this trip who were riding home in the rear flatbed of the small truck. Even they were picking up on the highly charged energies that were passing between he and I in the little cab of the truck. One of the times that we pulled over they even asked, "What the heck is going on in there?! We can feel it back here!"

When we reached my apartment, we said our goodbyes as if nothing had happened.

We had a number of business dealings together and shortly after the day of the ride from the Sacred Valley, he came by my apartment to discuss some business. I will admit that I was hoping that things would go deeper with him, and I was a little nervous. He did have another romantic commitment which was the reason that things had not progressed with us thus far. We were sitting on the sofa in my living room, and I was stammering my way through what it was I wanted to say when he stood up, took my hand, and led me into my bedroom. He sat me on the bed and said, "Now, Lisa, tell me what you want to say." Our eyes met and in silence he pushed me back on the bed and started kissing me with absolute ravenous passion. Within seconds his hands were everywhere, up my shirt, down my pants, and it was everything that sex normally is except for the fact that he was still fully dressed. I was so stunned that I didn't quite know what to do.

I thought, "This is certainly not what I had in mind, but at this stage I don't know if it would even be possible to stop him. It would be like trying to stop a freight train going at full speed." It was as if his consciousness had left his body, and he was no longer the sweet friend that he had been for the previous four months, but was a fireball of male hormones that had lost control.

In truth, it was virtually a sexual assault. After about 45 seconds he had to come up for air, so to speak, and I caught his gaze and looked deeply into his eyes to try to get his attention. I swear, I saw his consciousness come back into his body.

A look of recognition came across his face and he said, "WHAT AM I DOING??! Oh my God, I am SO sorry. What am I doing?!! You can't undo these things!!"

We sat back up on the edge of the bed, dazed by the tsunami of energy that had just been unleashed. He looked at me and, with an expression of absolute terror on his face, stood up and exclaimed, "You're Medusa!!" and went to flee my apartment. I went after him and caught him by the hand in the living room and yanked him down on the sofa.

"I am NOT Medusa! You sit down here! YOU are going to take responsibility for your actions and your role in this. I am not saying that I didn't want that to happen, but you are not going to project on to me, as a woman, your lack of self-control!"

Needless to say, that was the end of that. I realized that though I had known this man for four months and in that four months he had never once made a reference to the Catholic Church, and as a matter of fact, had demonstrated his deep dedication to the Andean shamanic path, that what had happened there was that I'd very nearly ended up in bed with the Catholic church. No, thank you!!

That was the extent of my personal romantic experience with Cusqueñean men.

After my birthday introduction to the Cusco nightlife, I started going out more often. The live music in Cusco is abundant and, for the most part very good. There are also plenty of discotheques and clubs. Cusco is a bit of a party destination for many people coming from other parts of Peru and the rest of the world and certainly for the tourists that flock here. There were many places that didn't really suit me, but I had found one band in particular that I really enjoyed. I loved their music which was powerful and upbeat. For the first time in decades, I felt comfortable dancing in public. I loved, loved, loved to dance to their music! It was just my rhythm, and I learned to let the music inside me and just let it move me. I felt so much joy and so much energy after their 90 minute set that I would come home at 1:00 in the morning and lie in bed, and I couldn't even sleep because of the smile that was plastered across my face.

I never thought it would be possible for me to feel this happy again. They didn't play in the same venue all the time, but switched from night to night to different locations. I would go out to watch them and dance a couple of times a week, when I didn't have to wake up at the crack of dawn the next day.

This is where it became apparent that I was considered to be quite attractive by some of the beautiful young men who also enjoyed this band. I was kinda liking it…

The Gringa Hunters - Bricheros/Bricheras

What is a brichero/brichera? Never have I lived in a place that has a special, well-known and recognized social category for people who use other people to improve their lifestyles. Yes, I am told that this goes on in many cultures around the world, but this was my first hands-on experience with it.

When I joined my first Spanish class in Peru, during the Orientation, we were told about bricheros/as. We were told to be wary of them.

A brichero/a is a Peruvian who uses tourists in one of two ways.

First, as a ticket to get out of Peru. The word comes from the word "bridge," and that is what they are looking for, a bridge out of their station in life to a better life–preferably somewhere else besides Peru. The goal is to get the tourist or foreigner to fall in love with them and take them away. If it is a brichera (female) you are dealing with, be sure not to have unprotected sex, as her goal is likely to get pregnant since that is an excellent opportunity to hook a responsible-minded foreigner into either marriage or many years of child-support payments.

Failing that, the brichero/a will settle for a couple of days or weeks of improved lifestyle while still here in Peru–food, drinks, sex, perhaps drugs and if they are really lucky, a bit of travel. I asked a Peruvian friend of mine to define what a brichero is, and he said, "Someone who steals from you without you realizing it."

The trick is that bricheros and bricheras are EXTREMELY charismatic. They are usually very good-looking, charming and personable. They absolutely know how to "play" you, no matter who you are. And there are a LOT of them in Cusco.

Cusco has a reputation as being a bit of a party destination for Peruvians and foreigners alike. There are lots of bars, and lots of dancing and drinking and drugging. The people who are in Cusco for a long weekend are just looking to have a good time, and that often means a sexual fling while they are out of their own territory. And the brichero is there to help make that dream come true. The word they use for "scoring" with a gringa/o is making a *conquista*–conquest.

Living in Cusco long enough to watch it all in action, I knew who some of the players were. There were some extremely attractive young men who expressed an interest in me. One brichero had come after me on a number of occasions. Well, what older woman would not be tempted by a beautiful young man who makes her feel like the center of the universe, even if just for an evening or two? We would dance and he would seduce me in every moment of that dance. He would come sit with me, really close, and one time, in an instant his hand was down the back of my jeans, cupping the cheek of my ass.

I will not say that I was completely taken aback by this bold and brazen move. And I will also not say that I was not a little tempted and excited by it as well.

"Yes," you say, "But don't you ask yourself 'Why? Why would a gorgeous young man be attracted to a woman twice his age?'" And the truth is, no, you don't ask, because for a fleeting moment you forget that you are no longer 25, and you want to believe that he really is interested in you. YOU. Not your money, or drinks or sex, but YOU. Yes, it is completely delusional, but we humans can be very good at that…

Well, I am not one to act on impulse, so I did not go with him. I watched and asked around, only to find out that he had been having an affair with an acquaintance of mine for some time. I asked her about him. She said, "Go ahead if you want, just be sure you know that he is a brichero. He will be asking you for drinks and money all the time."

By the way, that is the dead giveaway to knowing that you are dealing with a brichero/a. They will never offer to pay for anything.

That took all the air out of my balloon. I did NOT need another child and it felt downright creepy to me. That was certainly NOT what I was looking for.

The problem, as I see it, is the level of dishonesty involved. Prostitution is, at least an honest profession. This is a form of prostitution, but there is much deceit around it–they are frequently professing love, fate, destiny, and a weaving of a fabric of romance which is not true.

There are various levels of this as well. I never saw this myself but I am told that this can go very deep. There are people who go to foreign places who are perhaps lacking self-esteem and can become easy targets for these bricheros/bricheras that prey upon them. Coming from another culture, they are not accustomed to being targeted like this, and don't know how to recognize it. These predators invade their space in ways in which they are not accustomed, and next thing they know they have fallen hook, line and sinker. One friend told me that he was at Western Union, and he saw the bricheras all in there, waiting for money that was flowing in from various "stooges."

I am also told that the native people hold these imposters in great disdain, and even treat them with hostility, given the opportunity, at soiling the reputation of their countrymen.

There is even a book written in Peru called "The Gringa Hunter" (in Spanish it is *El Cazador de Gringas)* by Mario Guevana Paredes. It is required reading for all of my longer-term guests.

They come away saying, "I didn't like that story very much." To which I respond, "It was not meant to be read for enjoyment. You need to understand what goes on here. No judgment if you choose to step into it. Just so you know what is what. " (Peru is certainly not the only place in the world where this goes on. It happens all over the world in varying degrees of sophistication.)

In the story, the author sees being a brichero as a profession, and one with lots of competition. He knows that he is looked down upon by others, but the way he sees it, he is using his wits to improve his life. He does not hold his targets in very high esteem. There is a sense of entitlement that he feels, that his targets are so much better off than he, and that by giving them a little Latin Love–which he maintains is a valuable commodity that they are in search of–he can better his life. He sees no harm in this.

Here is an excerpt from his book:

> *She was sitting by herself at one of the tables, captivated by the ignoramuses playing an Andean song. Let me tell you, she impressed me a lot and I had been flat broke for days. Nowadays money doesn't go very far and I hadn't had a buck since the North American girl I lived with for several months left. She was something worth seeing. She was so crazy in love with me that she promised to send me a plane ticket to visit her. Experience has taught me that only fools believe those promises. But I can't complain about the months we spent together. I had a woman who looked like a model, a room in a downtown motel, and the best food. My pockets were always bulging with money and all that just for giving her a bit of love.*
>
> *…I saw her and immediately approached her table. In this profession the competition is fierce. Nowadays any brichero can beat you to it by a little and fuck you over, because the chances of scoring the gringa are reduced to zero. In addition, last night's gringa was Nordic. I'm not going to lie to you. Wherever she was from, I would've made her fall in love with me. You know, I'd spent days like a hunter on the prowl hanging around the places where gringas go: small plazas, coffee shops, taverns and archeological sites, until last night when I finally saw her.*
>
> *….Well, I'll tell you. I used an old trick with the gringa that's always worked. It was to convince her that our meeting wasn't by chance, but rather it was due to the magnetism this city radiates, making it possible for us to meet, because she's been in my dreams for a long time…I told her that as a novice of the practices of the knowledge of the magical Andean world, I had another way of perceiving reality…my perception came from an ancient belief that only belonged to the chosen ones. To be chosen meant to have passed through different stages of*

138

knowledge, in which the overcoming of one's affections for material things is one of our principal qualities.

Well, what a load of horseshit!

****

All this can blur the lines a bit and be the cause for some confusion. There was another attractive young man who expressed an interest in me. I would see him every couple of months when I was out dancing. Invariably, he would come join me on the dance floor. He lived in another far away town and came into Cusco occasionally for business. He asked me if I would consider seeing him. I told him I was not interested in being his "Cusco stop," I wanted more from a relationship than that. He said to me, "You know I am not a brichero. I am a professional and have a university degree."

"Well, that is lovely, but, I'm sorry, it doesn't work for me".

This went on for a couple of years. I finally pulled him aside one night and said, "Why me? Why are you after me for all this time? I am a quite a bit older than you…" His response took me aback.

He said, "This has nothing to do with age. This is something of the spirit." Well, my radar was definitely up, but I felt a sincerity in his response which intrigued me.

Shortly thereafter, he moved back to Cusco. In the next year, I learned that, indeed, he was not a brichero, and that he was sincere. We became very good friends, and it had absolutely nothing to do with him trying to better his station in life.

It was just one of those odd circumstances where two people from completely different walks of life and time become deeply connected in friendship. (Though defining the "terms" of that friendship did require some fine tuning…) Indeed, I saw occasions where being a gringa actually worked against me.

I could sense, at times, that some men I met just did not want to have to deal with the social stigma of being with a foreigner and all that entails. Or perhaps he identified more with his indigenous roots, and therefore was consciously choosing that path.

Pachamama and Women in the Andes

Pachamama/Mother Earth is the representation of the divine feminine in the Andes, and women are considered to be a part of her body. The Andean women are round in shape and are frequently represented by carved gourds, round and plump, with long black braids. They wear such full skirts that it isn't even apparent when they are pregnant. One day they just turn up with a baby in their arms. In agrarian communities, the women sit on the ground, close to the earth–they *are* Pachamama. The men stand, closer to the sun, which represents the divine masculine. This is the way it is. Potatoes are feminine and grow within the body of Pachamama, corn stalks are masculine and reach for the sun.

Everything is seen as divine complements, which they call *yanantin/masintin*. One cannot exist without the other. They are not opposites, they are *complements*. To plant a field with potatoes, a man and a woman are both supposed to be present. There are things that the men do, and other things that the women do. The men dig the holes. The women put the seed in the body of Pachamama, cover the hole, and then stamp the soil down with their feet. This practice is not about gender roles, but rather, it is about honoring the sacred relationship that human beings have with Pachamama and the world in which they live.

In ancient times it was the women who were in charge of selecting the seed potatoes. Peruvians owe their incredible genetic diversity of potatoes to the women. There are over 3,000 varieties of potatoes in Peru.

The gender roles in Peru tend to be more traditional. The role of the women in the countryside is to have babies and take care of the family. This is considered to be a natural cycle and natural role. The indigenous women are very hardworking, can be downright fierce, and are very loyal to their families. They remind me of mama bears. They are so dedicated and giving to

141

you if you are considered a part of their family. But if you cross them, watch out!

The conflict that comes in for me is the matter of choice. I grew up in a society where I had a choice, and I chose to give birth to two children, and then I stopped. I imagine there is a surrender that comes when one has to accept that one's entire adult life will be spent in the various phases of pregnancy and raising children.

****

I would like to preface this next section by saying that the following are my impressions from my own limited personal experiences as I explored the fascinating and enigmatic topic of women in the Andes in the twenty-first century. Customs vary dramatically from other parts of Peru and also within different socio-economic strata. This is by no means meant to be exhaustive or complete as I found the women of the Andes to be very complex and multi-layered.

The women in the cities seem to have more of the Spanish influence. There is a fascinating concept that has been named in recent years *marianismo*. It is the feminine equivalent to machismo. *Marianismo* is the idea that women must conform and live up to the fully feminine ideal. It comes from the Catholic influence of the Virgin Mary or "Maria" who was considered pure and selfless—a virgin *and* a mother. In this concept, the ideal woman is eternally self-sacrificing and spiritually immaculate. It sees women as semi-divine, morally superior to and spiritually stronger than men. The traits of feminine passivity and sexual purity are very important. There is also power in the female ability to produce life. The valued feminine traits are that she is submissive, kind, instinctive, emotional, modest, virtuous, vulnerable, unassertive and sexually abstinent until after marriage. In *marianismo*, it is the bad woman who enjoys premarital sex, whereas the good woman only experiences it as a marriage requirement. Her status as a woman is elevated when she has children. She is a caring mother, religious and pious. I

142

have even heard it said that marriage to a woman in Peru can be like a religion unto itself. I have also heard it said that Peruvian women are "machista," helping to preserve the "macho" society themselves.

One woman told me that she was told by her mother that she was to accept her husband with all his weaknesses and never, ever mention them. She was told that she would be an actual part of him.

In *marianismo*, women are the ones who take care of the children and take care of the house by cleaning, cooking and serving the husband. However, the most emphasized role is as a mother, and the role of a wife is considered secondary by many. Parenthood is considered a higher priority than partnership. Perhaps this is because of the requirement of women to be obedient to their husbands which, of course, makes it harder to find equal ground in a partnership. This role is deeply ingrained in many of the Latin American cultures, and many of the women accept it as their way of life.

This is one concept that I found that helped me to better understand some of what I was seeing. I would like to point out that it is not a well-known concept, and the Peruvian girlfriends that I shared it with were not familiar with it, though they agreed that they had been affected by it to varying degrees. They wanted to be sure that I was aware that there are many other trends in Peruvian society amongst the people in the cities, and the younger generation. And, of course, different socio-economic levels of society are affected differently, as well.

There are so many things that come into play, and I don't pretend to understand or even be familiar with them all. However, from what I have seen in my experiences over my years in Peru, generally speaking, the roles do tend to be more traditional than I have seen in my experiences in the U.S. and Europe. As a personal example, within my own family there have been a couple of cases of role reversal within marriages, with the man being the stay-at-home parent and the woman being the primary breadwinner. Not once in my time in Peru did I see a Peruvian man taking primary responsibility for childcare.

One time I was with an American girlfriend in a café chatting with a very highly-regarded and well-educated man that we knew who was in his 70's and had a background in Anthropology. I thought this was an amazing opportunity to speak to a native Peruvian about some of the concepts and attitudes I was coming across to try to get some perspective and clarity around them, since he spoke excellent English. We were sharing with him our views of the role of women and particularly of our own lives and how we have chosen to live them. My girlfriend was in her forties and had chosen not to have children.

He looked at her, wide-eyed and said, "You don't want children?? You don't want children! Now *that* is a problem! *That* is a problem!!" He truly perceived our choices as a total breakdown of society. It was most enlightening. We both came away feeling very grateful that we had been raised in a society where we had choices.

In truth, I feel that my personal experience with Peruvian women has been somewhat limited. When I have attempted closer relationships with them I have always felt that they were holding me at arm's length. Perhaps it is because I am a foreigner. I always feel that they are sweet to my face, but that it is a bit disingenuous, and that when they turn their backs they just roll their eyes.

I come from a family and society that is pretty direct. My mind really just doesn't work that well at seeing it when others are not straightforward. I come away from my interactions feeling like I don't understand what has transpired, kind of like I am a bug that has landed in a spider web. Though I do have personal relationships with a few Peruvian girlfriends, they tend to be people who have traveled or lived abroad and have not conformed so much to traditional gender roles.

I have heard it said that the more macho the men in a society are, the more manipulative the women will be. The women that I have encountered have been extremely possessive with their men and very jealous of their men's interactions with other women. Given the behavior of the men, perhaps it is justified, but I haven't seen that it alters the men's actions in any way.

144

Male infidelity in marriage is very common where I was living in Cusco. The women hate it, and yet they do nothing to stop it. They don't see themselves as having any control over it. The women have survived so much subjugation, and it seems that they are overwhelmed by their past and this stops them from moving into or changing their future.

Even the language is peppered with words that point to the traditional attitudes towards the relationship between men and women. The word for girlfriend is *novia* which is actually the word for "bride." The word for pregnant is *embarasada*, which sounds suspiciously like "embarrassed." The woman who stays home and looks after it is held in very high regard, and she is called *esposa* which translates to "wife." It doesn't seem to matter whether the couple is married or not.

Esposa is spoken as a compliment, but it comes laden with all of the responsibilities that define this role in the social mind. One of my boyfriends insisted on calling me his *esposa*. I could see that he loved using this word–that it brought him some deep inner satisfaction to have an *esposa*.

To say that I was "gun shy" of being considered a "wife" after my own experience with marriage would be an understatement. I honestly doubted that I would ever want to become married again in anything vaguely representing a traditional marriage, so I resisted him calling me that for the first year of our relationship. He continued to use the term, and always with so much affection that eventually I thought *"What the heck, if it makes him so happy to use it, just let him use it."*

Soon I was finding him projecting onto me all of his definitions of how an *esposa* should behave–having meals ready for him, serving his plate, expecting me to be available to him whenever he turned up at any time of the day or night. When I called him out on it, his excuse was that for me to serve his plate was *cariñoso*–affectionate! Well, that role just didn't suit me at all. I had gone to a great deal of trouble to become single again. I ended up in a society where the word for girlfriend is "bride," and a boyfriend who insists on calling me his "wife".

I have discussed this with one of my Cusqueñean girlfriends who has spent much time abroad and she is as perplexed by the complexity of the roles of women in Peru as I am. She told me that before she had a child, her family was really not at all happy with her. She then got pregnant and had a child out of wedlock which, much to her surprise, elevated her status within the family! I don't imagine that Peruvian society and culture is the only one full of contradictions, but I found all this very challenging.

Once again, these are my own personal perceptions from my admittedly limited experiences with women in the Andes. Many of these ideas may actually be more global in nature and apply to women around the world and throughout the ages. Women have been (and still are) subjugated in many cultures. It is a very complex and multi-faceted issue.

Moche

After I broke things off with Pumita, I started making a conscious search for a new boyfriend. I had learned from Pumita several things that I did not want to repeat. I was ruling out men from Cusco for the most part, men who didn't seem to have the ability to respect my wishes and cultural differences, macho men, and anyone who appeared to be too ambitious. Discriminating by age was a little more difficult because so many of them were younger than I. If they enjoyed the same music that I did, Peruvian Tribal Fusion, and if they liked to dance, all the better. It was a good start. I was having a lot of fun, but I was looking for a longer-term relationship, which can be difficult in Cusco. It can be very transient in Cusco with so many people coming and going.

I would meet these prospective boyfriends in the clubs and we would dance. Then I always wanted to have "The Talk," where we would talk about what we were looking for and if we had enough in common to pursue things any further. Was he going to be in town for a while? Could he make eye contact with me and not be intimidated by my strong, independent personality? I must say it was really fun to feel so attractive, though I wasn't having a lot of luck in finding what I was looking for. I wanted a mature, mutually respectful relationship with a man who could honor my need for independence and also my lack of desire for any kind of traditional relationship that would include living together or getting married.

"I'm not going to do your laundry or look after any children," I would say. "I'm not a traditional woman, I am not into traditional roles. I want a respectful companionship and good sex. I don't mind paying my own way, but I won't pay for yours" (see chapter on Bricheros). That sent many of them running for the horizon, which was exactly what it was meant to do.

One night I was out and I had been running into a group of guys for the past couple of weeks that usually went out together. They were all musicians (I have a bit of a weakness for musicians) and they were all gorgeous–beautiful long, black Peruvian hair (I think long hair on men is soooo sexy). I was taking turns dancing with a couple of them. One was more my age, but he was obviously more interested in one of my girlfriends so I was talking with one of the younger ones. We got to the point of "The Talk" but he wouldn't look me in the eye, so that was not a good sign. One of the others wanted to chat with me, but it was difficult with the loud music and my poor Spanish, and he didn't dance, so it wasn't really going anywhere.

A day or two later one of my girlfriends who had been with me that night and knows me quite well came to me and said, "I hope you don't mind, I gave your phone number to someone. He was with us at the club the other night, and he asked me for your number."

Well, I didn't mind. It was the guy that had tried to chat with me, and though initially I didn't feel a strong attraction to him, he'd seemed like a nice enough guy, so I was willing to consider it. Plus he was more my age which eliminated a lot of the other complications that had been coming up with the younger ones.

One thing led to another and one night shortly thereafter we ended up making a date to have "The Talk" over lunch the next day. The conversation went exceedingly well. He was super sweet, super healthy, didn't have any addictions, didn't smoke weed, drank a little chicha (corn beer) occasionally but wasn't an alcoholic, and he ate meat (so do I and I don't like to feel like I have to apologize about it since there seem to be so many strict vegetarians around). He was in wonderful physical condition, already had a grown child and even a young grandchild. He didn't really care about getting married–as a matter of fact, he had been single for the past 20 years.

I soon learned that though he came across as fairly shy in public, that behind closed doors he became a fiery lover, and a very sexy, very sweet, affectionate man.

Will wonders never cease?!

Time passed and things were going very well with Moche and me. He was from the North of Peru, near Trujillo, where all those graphically sexual Pre-Inkan ceramics come from, and it appeared he'd been studying them. He really was very healthy and a phenomenal, erotic lover.

Behind closed doors he was all mine! I hadn't been so happy in decades! Being with him somehow made me more of who I was. He gave me an opening to express myself sexually in ways I had never known before. He made me more "me." He'd say to me, "*Eres muy mujer*" (You are such a woman) and he called me his "*Gatita ardiente*" (sex kitten).

He somehow managed to hit ALL my spots! I learned all kinds of things about myself. On more than one occasion in the bedroom I found myself asking "How the hell did I end up in THIS position??" He came up with things I had never heard of or seen in any book. When we were together like this there was no time or space for me. I had been transported to another world, floating in the clouds of glorious sensation.

He was not a big man, not much taller than me, but he was lean and solid muscle–and very strong. He had beautiful, long wavy blue black hair, known in Peru as *negro azabache*. One time I asked him if he put something on his hair to make it that amazing blue black color. He turned and looked at me gazing squarely into my eyes and said with pride, "Soy un hombre natural." (I am a natural man.) That was his tagline for me. He wouldn't put anything in his mouth that he deemed to be anything less than healthy, and it was paying off.

Ten years earlier I genuinely didn't care if I ever had sex again in my life. And here I was–reborn, liberated and more sexually fulfilled than I'd been since I first got married a very long time ago!

****

Sometimes we would just lie there in bed with him holding me, spooning. Oh my God, how I had missed spooning! For years and years I'd only been able to spoon with my children, but being the parent, of course I was always the outside spoon. This man would wrap his arms and legs around me in such a sweet way and just hold me, and I got to be the inside spoon. So lovely! Our bodies were such a perfect fit. I felt his sweet, warm love wrap around me in such an embracing way, not possessive–just holding space for what we were sharing.

I don't know that I'd ever felt this before, this unconditional, undemanding love. About eight months after we started our relationship, we were going to be apart for a few months since we were both traveling. When you have something so good, sometimes the fear of losing it creeps in. I had been unwilling to communicate that with him earlier, even pushing him away at times, perhaps for fear of losing him and grasping for what I perceived as some shred of control by being the one who was leaving rather than the one who was being left.

I got really brave one time, and as we were lying together, I allowed those feelings to come through. I was lying on my side with Moche behind me, holding me. Tears started to leak from my eyes. Though I wasn't really crying–my breathing had not changed, the tears continued to flow. As I allowed these emotions to come through, I just observed how the tears would flow out of one eye, pool in the space on the side of my nose until there were enough and then they would flow over the bridge of my nose and through the other eye, eventually ending up on the pillowcase.

From the position we were in, Moche could not see my face, but after a while he said to me, "Are you crying?"

I nodded my head and he asked me, *"Porque, mi amor?"* (Why, my love?)

I took a deep breath and I decided to be braver still and to tell him why I was crying. I told him that he was very special to me, that no one had ever loved me the way that he loved me. I told him that I loved the way that he loved me for being who I am and not trying to change me. And I loved the way that when I said something he didn't expect to hear me say, he would just cut his eyes over to my general direction without turning his head. I loved the way he flinched whenever he took the first sip of something that was really cold. I told him that I loved his long fingers and toes. I loved the way he wrapped himself around me and the way our long hair would get all tangled up in each other's while we were making love and we'd have to stop and sort out whose hair was whose. I loved that he was such a different man behind closed doors and that I was the lucky recipient of that part of his being. And then I got the courage to tell him that I was afraid of losing that. I told him that I had suffered so much in the past and that I was tired of suffering and I was so grateful to him for giving me the opportunity to feel the love that we shared. By then I really was crying, and I just let that emotion flow through me for a long time. I blew my nose, and then I cried some more.

Moche just held me. He held that space for me without trying to stop me from crying, without trying to cheer me up or distract me. He just kept his beautiful brown, lean body entwined around mine and he held me. He said one thing.

He said, "This is what we do—we live, we suffer, and we love."

****

When he slept, Moche was so still and so quiet that sometimes I would forget he was even there. I could barely hear him breathing. I could be lying next to him and not even be in the mood for sex but it was like my body was willing his body to become one with mine. I had never had that experience before. It was so sweet, so incredibly sweet. I thought to myself how

151

blessed I was to have the opportunity to share this intimacy with another being.

Things went really well for several months. But eventually the endorphins wore off and the challenges came up for us to work through, as in any relationship. There was just one big problem for me—his Peruvian sense of time.

My gringa girlfriends and I talk about this endlessly. The Peruvian sense of time is so different from a Western culture sense of time. We tend to do what we say we are going to do, when we say we are going to do it. To us this is a reflection of our own personal integrity.

Peruvians, being eager to please, tell you what you want to hear in that moment and you are supposed to understand that that's what they're doing. They don't want to disappoint you. They have absolutely no problem with not doing what they say they're going to do when they say they're going to do it, or possibly, not doing it at all. For me, it is the single most frustrating aspect of this culture.

Let me give an example: Some friends had asked me to housesit while they were traveling. I asked Moche if he would come spend the first night with me so I wasn't in a strange house all alone, which he happily agreed to do. He was working until 9:00 p.m. At nine he called me and said, "I'm on my way, I'll be there in 15 minutes." Well, everyone knows that Latinos are late, right? He didn't know exactly where I was staying, though he knew more or less where the house was. So by 9:30 I thought, "Okay, here I am in my sexy lingerie with my favorite music on, a glass of wine in my hand, and looking forward to the privacy and time to spend with him alone (I had a roommate in my apartment at the time whose schedule we always had to work around). He makes me wait, so I'll make him wait." And I refused to look out the window to show him where I was until 9:45. At 9:45, he still wasn't there, so I called him. He told me that he had run into a friend on the street, and they were quickly getting a bite to eat. He would be with me in 15 minutes. 45 minutes later, at 10:30 I called him again. I told him that I was tired of waiting, and I was very upset–it would really be best if he didn't come. He said he was sorry, but they'd ordered a pizza and "You know how long it takes to make pizza here. I'll be there in 15 minutes." I said, "Don't come. It is too late now and I am very upset," and I hung up the phone. I sent him a text just to make sure that he knew that I had said not to come. I took a Xanax, turned off my phone and went to bed. I was very hurt, disappointed and so upset by that stage that if I had seen him it would not have been good.

When I got up the next morning, I had nine missed calls and texts from him. I was still very upset and did not want to see him. He was going to Bolivia that day to pick up some musical instruments and he sent me a text in the morning asking me what had happened, which I chose to ignore. How could he possibly not know what had happened? He had come by the house after our last call and waited outside for me until sometime after midnight which I found very hard to understand considering I had told him and texted him not to come.

He sent me a text in the afternoon saying that he was leaving for Bolivia, to which I responded, "Adios."

Within a couple of days, I had a girlfriend come visit me from the U.S. and we went traveling to the North of Peru together for two weeks. So I was pretty well distracted by that trip, and Moche and I didn't have any communication at all for the next three weeks. When I got back from my travels, I was really missing him. Meeting him in my apartment was not a possibility because now I had not only a roommate but also a houseguest, so I called him and asked him if he would meet with me in a nearby hotel, which he did. I asked him why he hadn't made an attempt to contact me, and he said, "I was waiting for you to calm down."

He seemed very hurt. We talked things through, and I explained, at great length, why I was so upset to be left waiting for so long, so late at night. By the time he would've gotten there the night would have been over. I was hoping to spend time alone with him and just have some lovely private time together.

153

He had, in my mind, traded me in for a pizza. I found it very offensive. We made up that afternoon. We made love, and I invited him to come again to spend the night with me that night in the hotel.

I didn't hear back from him that night, which under the circumstances, hurt my feelings, though I can't say I was completely surprised by it. With Peruvians, you learn to make plans B and C since plan A so frequently just doesn't happen. You find yourself trying not to get your hopes up so that you don't get disappointed, but it is quite a quandary. None of the gringas that I've spoken to here have mastered it.

I was messaging him the next day on the internet, and I made some kind of comment about wondering if he'd traded me in for a pizza again the night before, when he didn't return to see me. He asked me why I was saying these things, and I explained, as I had many times before, that it didn't make me feel like I was very special when he was constantly putting other priorities ahead of seeing me, like someone he had run into on the street, or stopping for a meal on the way to see me, and any other number of less-than-acceptable-to-me excuses for always being late.

His response to that was, "Hee-hee-hee" which triggered in me a very strong emotional response. I responded, "FUCK OFF, MOCHE!!!!" in English, which was the most offensive thing I could think of to say at that moment, and I closed down my computer.

I said to myself, "That's it, I'm done! How could I have just explained my feelings yesterday, which were so strong that it nearly ended our relationship and now he's doing the exact same thing again today?"

Shortly thereafter, I ran into an American friend who is a retired therapist and has been married to a Peruvian for some years. Admittedly, I was beside myself with frustration with what I deemed as his unacceptable behavior. She and I were having lunch together and I was going on and on and on endlessly about my frustration. My friend first laughed in my face, and then told me that my expectations were completely unrealistic for Peru.

154

She then offered to give me a very good price for some therapy to help me work through this. Her help was invaluable at helping me understand that this was a cultural difference and not an attack on my personal value, which is how I had been perceiving it.

It was about a month before I saw Moche again. Things went much better with us when I stopped becoming so upset about something that is a completely acceptable cultural norm in Peru. I am not saying that it doesn't still frustrate me, but it is insane to keep doing the same thing over and over again and expecting different results. When in Rome, do as the Romans do, right?

****

Moche and I were sitting on the sofa in my living room one afternoon after we'd gotten back together, when he turned to me and asked, "What means 'Fuck off'? I asked my roommate what it means and he didn't know either. He said, 'Well, she's a gringa, and you know they get upset easily. I guess she was upset....' I know what 'fuck you' means but what means 'fuck off'?"

Well I just about split my sides laughing. That was so funny to me on so many levels–that I could say the most offensive thing I could possibly think of in that moment, and he just shrugged his shoulders and had no idea what I was talking about. One of the ongoing, ridiculous outcomes of trying to communicate with someone from a different culture when most of the time you really have no idea what the hell is going on. For weeks after that one of us would just mutter, "What means fuck off?" and we would just laugh and laugh at ourselves.

At one point, Moche decided he wanted to learn more English. He asked me, "What does 'shoshosho' mean?"

"I have no idea, where did you hear that?"

So he wrote it down for me. This is what he wrote:

XOXOXO

Then he asked me, "What does 'ah way sew may' mean?"

"I really have no idea what you are saying, Moche."

"Yes, you do! They use it all the time!"

"OK, write it for me."

A-W-E-S-O-M-E was what he wrote. "See? Ah-way-sew-may!!"

We spent a lot of time laughing at learning each other's languages!

****

Who knows what the future holds? I stopped making long-term plans after my marriage ended and my lifetime of plans flew out the window. However, I also thought I may never again have the opportunity to share this level of intimacy with another man. For this opportunity, I am deeply grateful!

Part 4

My Journey on the Andean Spiritual Path

The Q'ero

The beautiful young man with brown skin and a pointed hat dripping in tiny white beads and brightly colored tassels put his hand on his heart and bowed slightly. With his eyes closed he said, "Urpichay Sonqochay."

"Doves fly in my heart" is the way he told me "thank you."

Juan Quispe was 24 years old at the time. I was speechless, a rare condition for me. Cultural anthropology had always fascinated me. Although I had never formally studied it except for one course in college, I considered myself to be an amateur cultural anthropologist. I always studied in whatever way possible, be it traveling, living in another culture, watching documentaries or reading about it from books. My favorite travels were when I found myself completely immersed in another culture–whether in a boat on the klongs of Thailand, or with the virtually naked Choco Indians in the Darien jungle or in a Candomble/Santeria ceremony in Brazil.

And here I was standing face-to-face with a Q'ero shaman who was telling me that doves flew in his heart because of something I had done.

****

The first time I ever met the Q'ero was my very first night in Cusco, in November 2005. Our guide, Jorge, had invited them to come join us for dinner. It might have been a propitious meeting, but my head was spinning from our whirlwind trip down to the Southern Hemisphere. I was at over 11,000 feet above sea level for the first time in my life, and it was bucketing rain. We were in a restaurant in the main plaza of Cusco.

What I saw were two young men in colorful native attire, and they were hoping to sell some of the beautiful hand-woven textiles for which they are well-known. I didn't even have enough oxygen in my brain to count. All I wanted to do at that stage was get to my hotel and go to bed. Years later, I did get to know both of these Q'ero quite well.

It was 3 years later before the timing was right for me. In late 2008, when I brought my son and first group to Cusco and we were staying at Lesley's hostel, she introduced me to Juan Quispe Calcina. Lesley is godmother to one of his children, and one of the ways she helped to support his family was by allowing them to come to her hostel to sell their textiles. Roger and I both got a serious "hit" off of this first encounter.

Juan's energy was like nothing I had ever encountered before. He was so open and pure, beautiful and deeply humble. The name, Quispe, is the Quechua word for crystal. He was looking to raise money to help build a school for his tiny village–a place so remote that Google Maps had marked that area as "Insufficient Data." At the time, the children had to leave their families Monday through Friday, as Juan did when he was young, to make the several hour trip to the nearest school to get an education. Juan had to travel for three or four days from where he lived to get to Cusco, to try to earn money to buy the materials to build the school. They used no money in Q'eros, and the stores don't trade books for their currency of potatoes and alpacas, so they had to come to the city to earn money.

Roger and I were completely dazed when Juan had gone, left in the wake of what felt to us a potentially life-changing encounter. Lesley then shared with us a documentary film that she had that had been made about the Q'ero. The connection was made. Juan was present off and on during that trip, but it wasn't until I returned to Cusco to live in April of 2011 that our relationship deepened.

When I was a manager at the boutique hotel, Juan would come in to do cleansing ceremonies for the hotel and sometimes for the guests. My relationship with Juan always felt oddly familial, like a long lost relative.

One day Juan told me that he was going for his daughter's first haircut the next day, and asked if I would come with him? I thought, "Oh, how sweet that he is nervous to do this alone and is asking me to come with him." I imagined us sitting in a salon looking on as someone else cut her hair.

But something told me that this was not what it appeared to be. I asked around and learned that, in fact, Juan was inviting me to become a part of his family. The person who does a child's first haircut becomes a Godparent, and has family-member status (more about that later).

Shortly thereafter, Juan invited me to come to his wedding up in Q'eros. Not just anyone gets to go to Q'eros, you must have an invitation. At the time there was no electricity, let alone hotels or restaurants up there. When Juan asked me, I felt tears prick the back of my eyelids–this was a dream come true for me!

Then I invited Juan to my birthday celebration, only to learn that he couldn't come because he had other plans already. We shared the same birthdate, just like my biological little brother!

Okay, that sealed it–Juan became my "little brother" that day!

****

So, who are the Q'ero? Who are these beautiful people that live in the mist and the cold, surrounded by the mountain spirits?

Some say that Q'eros was founded by Manco Ccapaq while he was searching for a place to found the imperial city of Cusco. According to legend, he was the son of the Sun and the Moon. He came out of the Lake Titicaca area and went first to Q'eros before choosing Cusco to build as his Imperial City. The Q'ero were the sacred weavers of the Inka Empire.

According to their oral history, the Spanish did come up once to try to kill them, but they enlisted the help of the powerful *apus*–the mountain spirits–who created a landslide that killed all of the Spaniards except one, so he could go back and tell the others. The Spanish left them alone after that.

It is cold and wet in Q'eros, and the air is rarified. Until the past few decades, they have lived exclusively on alpaca and potatoes, and some corn which they grow in patches a little

161

further down the mountainside toward the jungle. They have only recently decided it was time that they come down from their homes in the clouds. They are very physically strong people, and though their infant mortality rate is astronomically high, the ones that do survive can go barefoot in the cold, see in the dark, and work very, very hard under the harshest of conditions.

And yet they are very gentle people who never raise their voices, who embrace their children with such love and acceptance, and have such a strong sense of who they are–the few remaining direct descendants of the Inka. They have such a powerful cosmology and understanding of energies and the world in which they live that books have recently been written about them, and they have been referred to as the Masters of the Living Energy. They are always humble, with a child-like innocence, and with the deepest gratitude of any kindness that is extended to them. They take nothing for granted. In their harsh world where half of their babies never make it to their first birthday (which I was soon to witness myself firsthand), they learn that life is a fleeting gift. I am awestruck by their beautiful, mystical and powerful belief system that honors every single living thing, seen or unseen, and their steadfast love of *Pachamama*. And to the Q'ero, everything is a sentient, conscious being. Mother Earth is *Pachamama* who loves us and sustains us in so many ways, the Sun is *Inti Tayta* who shares divine light with us and allows life to continue on Earth, the Moon is *Mama Killa* and the Ocean is *Mama Cocha*. The stones speak, the weather will follow their command at times, coca leaves and fire take their prayers up to the *hanaq pacha*, the upper world where the energies are refined and where beings of light reside. There is no hell in their belief system and not even a word for evil in Quechua. Things are either "good" or "needs good."

I feel the deepest respect for these people. I feel so honored that they invited me into their world. They are elegant survivors–strong, humble and proud of who they are. Benito Machacca Apaza, a past President of Hatun Q'eros, has a gorgeous, happy face, full of character and he is Juan's godfather. He actually stopped a National Geographic Genographic project of collecting DNA samples from the Q'ero communities. NatGeo was baffled by this and said, "But you can know who your ancestors are!" To which he replied: "The Q'ero Nation knows that its history, its past, present, and future, is our Inka culture, and we don't need research called "genetics" to know who we are. We are Inkas, always have been and always will be."

The Basics of the Andean Cosmology

I stepped onto this path in earnest in that first meeting with Juan Quispe, when I bought a handwoven *mestana* from him. A *mestana* is a ceremonial cloth that is used for their sacred bundles, which they call a *mesa* (or sometimes a *misa*). This bundle is filled with sacred objects. In their tradition these are usually stones (*khuyas*) collected from the sacred mountains they have visited, or that have been gifted to them as initiation stones by their teachers. *Mesa* in Spanish means *table,* so a *mesa* is like a portable altar.

It took me a few years to learn and understand the teachings of this path well, but once I did, it fit me perfectly! Finally, I had found my spiritual path! Several books have been written that go into great detail about these teachings, and my favorites can be found in the Recommended Reading section at the back of this book. I will touch on the basics here, and if this appeals to you, you can go more deeply into it with these other excellent books.

The most fundamental concept in the Andean spiritual path is that of *ayni*. Ayni is the concept of sacred reciprocity, that everything in the world is interconnected, and that as you give, you must also receive. This concept is not just in material items, but also energetically. Most of their ceremonies are in honor of this. A beautiful representation of this is seen before each meal, when a drop of whatever they are about to drink is deliberately spilled from their cup onto the ground, to give back to Mother Earth/*Pachamama* a bit of what she has given us, a lovely and constant remembrance.

Everything in their world has Spirit. The world is alive, and you are never alone. They call this living energy *kawsay* (in other traditions it is known as *prana* or *chi.*) Kawsay is shared through intention and breath. When you use words, you are using a combination of your intention and your breath to call in these energies. When you blow onto coca leaves, you are putting your *kawsay* on them, and they act as messengers to carry your prayers where you want them to go. Your *kawsay* body is a bubble of energy which surrounds your physical body which they call your *poq'po* (Quechua for bubble). This is also known in other traditions as the *aura*.

The practitioners of the Andean spiritual path refer to themselves as *paqos* (initiates). They believe that there are basically two types of energy, and one of the key jobs of a *paqo* is to help transmute these energies in a healthy way. (They also frequently do healing work, work with herbs, and do readings with coca leaves.)

There is a refined, healthy energy that is natural in the world that they call *sami*. Sami is unlimited in the world, there is never a shortage of it, and it flows naturally through everything. *Sami* translates literally to "nectar" in the Quechua language. *Sami* is the nectar of life.

There is another energy which is created only by human beings. It is caused when the flow of *sami* is impeded, and the energy becomes stuck and heavy as a result. This energy is called *hucha*. We humans create this with our attachment to the way we think things ought to be, principally through fear, guilt, jealousy, anger and similar emotions. When we hold on to the energies we create with these emotions, they can manifest into physical illness, bad luck, and other undesirable things. When we fail to honor the *ayni* that is shared with us by giving something back, it can interrupt the natural flow of energy. *Hucha* is not bad, it is just misguided and not healthy for us. The goal is to keep your energy body as clean and light as possible.

There are three types of *paqos* and they are known as *pampamisayoqs, altomisayoqs,* and *kurak akulleqs.*

Kurak akulleqs are considered the highest level and work with beings from the upper world, or *hanaq pacha*. *Altomisayoqs* are the next level, and they are sometimes initiated into the role by being struck by lightning, not once, but three times. They work mostly with the *apus* (mountain spirits) and the energies of *Pachamama* (Mother Earth). Usually the male *paqos* call in the *apus* and the female *paqos* call in *Pachamama*. It is an extremely demanding role energetically, and most people don't want it. It is even said that being an *altomisayoq* makes it likely that you will have a shortened lifespan.

A *pampamisayoq* works with the Earth energies.

For all *paqos*, one of his/her key jobs is to help people transmute *hucha* into *sami*. They do this principally through ceremonies called *haywarikwee* (Quechua for "to offer with one's hands"–in Spanish they call them *despachos* or *pagos*) or *offerings to Mother Earth*. They take items from nature and create a beautiful mandala which is not only a work of art, but is an actual weaving of energies with these items which represent *ayni*, an exchange of energies with *Pachamama*, giving back to her what she so generously shares with us. *Despachos* can be very elaborate in places where many such items exist, or as simple as coca leaves and flowers infused with *kawsay,* the living energies of the people doing the ceremony, in places where not so much is available. The Q'ero are extremely practical people and masters at improvisation. They work with what they have.

One becomes a *pampamisayoq* over a period of years and through a series of initiations, or *karpays,* or by being in service to a more experienced *paqo*. This happens in a very specific *karpay* by a higher level *paqo* when an energetic transmission is given where you receive the entire lineage that person has to offer. Everyone who has been in that particular lineage is transferred to you during the *karpay*. They consider that they are activating the Inka seed within you (which is everyone's divine birthright) during the first of these initiations, which is strengthened in subsequent *karpays*. *Karpay* translates to "irrigation" in Quechua, and it is up to you to feed and irrigate that seed if you want it to germinate, grow and blossom. You do this by visiting the *apus*, working with your *mesa* on a regular basis, listening to the messages that you are given, and showing your dedication to this path by right living.

When they open their ceremonies, they call in all of the energies of the nature spirits, of which there are many. The two principle ones are *Pachamama* and the *apus.*

The Andean spiritual tradition believes that there are three worlds. *Hanaq pacha* is the Upper World. All of the celestial beings reside there, the most refined energies, the *apus*, all the celestial bodies and everything to do with the sky. *Hanaq pacha* is full of *sami*. They use the condor (and occasionally the hummingbird) to represent the *hanaq pacha* (p*acha* means the time/space continuum or "world").

The *kay pacha* is the world in which we live. *Kay pacha* is represented by the puma, and has both *sami* and *hucha*.

Ukhu pacha is the inner world. It is the rich, fertile Mother Earth, the place where all our food comes from, and where we put our ancestors when they die. It is the subconscious. There is no "hell" in their belief system. *Hucha* belongs in the *ukhu pacha,* where things are more dense. As with water, the deeper you go down, the higher the pressure. *Hucha* needs to flow down, like water does, into the denser world of the *ukhu pacha. Ukhu pacha* is represented by the snake.

When in Cusco, you will frequently see this trilogy of the condor, puma and snake together, to honor the three worlds.

Three is a sacred number for them. There are also three key principles in the Andean teachings which we need to integrate within ourselves to be healthy and balanced. They are *munay, yachay* and *llank'ay*—to feel, think and act.

Munay is the human power of a combination of deep love, beauty, and will, which to the Q'ero, are inseparable. *Munay* is the capacity to love and is what you feel when you look at a sunset that is so beautiful that you feel like you are being transformed by just looking at it. One of the deepest compliments I have ever received was when I was doing some work with my *mesa*, and a Q'ero came up behind me, and looking over my shoulder, he said, "*Munaycha."* (It is beautiful.)

Yachay best translates to "wisdom". It is considered to be the work of the mind, learning, superior consciousness, the ability to wisely use the knowledge gained through personal experience.

Llank'ay is of action and the physical body; it is the ability to perform physical labor, and also physical work in service to others, like helping plant their fields if one's neighbors are unable to do it themselves due to illness. An excellent example of *llank'ay* is moving rocks. There are a lot of rocks in Peru, so this is very fitting!

A *kintu* is a fan of three coca leaves, one representing each world and each principle. Whenever anyone wants to honor something, they take a *kintu* and put their *kawsay* on it with their breath, and either give it to another person, or leave it as an offering in the place they want to honor. *Kintus* are also a key item in *despacho* ceremonies.

****

These concepts are beautifully portrayed by the Andean Cross, in Quechua known as the *Chakana*, which is also seen as their Tree of Life.

This interesting geometrical shape encompasses an incredible amount of symbology. At the center is an empty circle, which is representative of Spirit and sometimes it is also referred to as the *qosqo*, the navel–where we are connected to our mother–*Pachamama*.

The shape is composed of a cross and a square. The square represents the four quarters of the Inka Empire, which they refer to as the *Tawantinsuyo*.

The three steps in each quarter are meant to be symbolic of the three worlds and the three key principles in the Andean Way. There are other various meanings as well, which vary depending on who you are talking to, in the typical fluid Peruvian manner.

The Andean cross is represented in some of the ancient ruins, frequently as only the top or bottom half of the full Andean cross. They can be seen in their entirety, carved into the stone at the top of the Inka ruins at Ollantaytambo and also in Bolivia at Tiwanaku.

The divine masculine is represented by *Inti Tayta,* Father Sun. The divine feminine is represented by *Mama Killa,* Mother Moon. The pairing of these two, as well as all concepts of duality (up/down, light/dark, day/night, man/woman) are considered complementary and a complete sacred couple. One cannot exist without the other. They do not have a word in their vocabulary for "opposite." Instead they use the word "complement." It is a subtle, and yet dramatic shift in perception. They call this concept *yanantin/masintin. Yanantin* means harmonious relationships between different beings (like man and woman), and *masintin* means harmonious relationships between similar beings (like two women). This is a beautiful depiction of the sacredness of differences.

Pachamama is a natural transmuter of energy. She mulches energy naturally, transmuting it from *hucha* into *sami.* She takes the waste products of animals and turns it into fertilizer which can create new life. There are places in nature which are natural spots to do this; for example, caves, natural rock outcroppings, lakes and springs. The Inka called these natural energy vortexes *wakas,* and they are excellent places to release *hucha,* and give it back to Pachamama. Many of their temples were built on top of the *wakas,* as they were honored for doing this important work. The *wakas* are all located on energetic ley lines in the Inka Empire, that they called *seqes.* They all emanate out of the spiritual center of the Inka Empire, the city of Cusco, more specifically out of The Temple of the Sun, known by the Inka as the *Q'oricancha*.

The Inka built ancient Cusco in the shape of a puma, the representation of the world in which we live, *kay pacha.* There are specific energetic points throughout the city, and temples are built on each one. They call these centers *ñawis* or "eyes," and though different from the chakras[6], they have a similar purpose in

---

[6] Chakras are energy points in the subtle body or aura. *Chakra* is the Sanskrit word for "wheel."

the energetic bodies of people and places. Cusco, which in Quechua is called *Qosqo,* translates to "navel," and it is believed to be the point where the Inka were most spiritually connected to their mother, *Pachamama.* There are other points in the city where they believe these other points are located.

One of the most famous of these *ñawis* is the head of the puma, which is in the place known as Saqsaywaman, one of the most sacred mountains/*apus* in the system. Saqsaywaman towers above Cusco, and phenomenal monolithic stones comprise it as a ceremonial center. No one today knows how they got those stones, weighing as much as 200 tons, into place. They are fitted together in a zigzag pattern like puzzle pieces, using no mortar. They are believed to represent the teeth of the puma.

One of the things that I find extremely appealing about the Andean spiritual path is its accessibility. They do not consider themselves special in any way–they are always humble. Their belief system is an open book to anyone who wants to learn it. As a matter of fact, if you know more than another person and they ask you, you are duty bound to share what you know with that person. When in the presence of another who has seniority in age or ability, they always defer with respect to their elder. Juan is normally the one conducting ceremonies, but when his father or uncle are around, Juan is the one carrying firewood, even though he is a better ceremonialist than some of the others. I have never witnessed a case of misplaced ego amongst them.

Westerners frequently refer to the practitioners of the Andean spiritual path as shamans. In truth, they are more mystics. Shamans tend to work between the worlds, using altered states of consciousness to access other realms and bring information back to this world. Frequently the goal of a shaman is to go beyond the human experience, into other dimensions. The Q'ero do not use Wachuma or Ayahuasca or altered states of consciousness to do their work, as is used is some forms of shamanism.

One of the goals of a *paqo* is not to transcend their humanity, but to become as fully human as possible, to connect with the energies of all the nature beings, to bring divinity into this world.

This work is not the solitary pursuit so frequently seen with shamanism. It is not just to be used for one's own personal transformation, but the idea is to bring it back to the community. They believe in pulling everyone up, in a truly social sense. They have no competitive sports in their tradition. They believe that as we get better through practicing *ayni,* and through right living, that we all evolve together.

As Joan Parisi Wilcox so eloquently said in sharing the teachings that came down to her from the Q'ero via her teacher, Juan Nuñez del Prado, in the movie *Q'ero Mystics of Peru (*by Seti Gershberg, 2014*):*

> *"It's not about having a supernatural experience. It's about having the truest natural experience that you can. It's about finding your true nature. The Judeo-Christian tradition tells us that we were all born in Original Sin. The Andean tradition tells us that we were all born with Original Virtue. We are all drops of the Mystery—when our parents came together and at that moment of conception, we were pulled from the Mystery. Each of us a single drop of the Mystery. In a sense our entire lives are a path of recovery and remembering, of bringing that core essence of who we are—which is divine— into the human and fully integrating it and interweaving it.*
>
> *That's a beautiful metaphor—that Q'ero are master weavers. For this kind of work we want to weave our energies, we want to weave our energies with other people, with our families, with our communities, with nature. We want to also remember that the essence, the pattern of that weaving, is ultimately that we are a part of the Mystery. So it's a path of recovery and remembering. It's not about learning anything, it's about remembering."*

One of the reasons that this belief system has endured, despite the Spanish/Catholics doing everything within their power to obliterate it, is that there is no one type of building or idol that they could destroy to weaken the impact of the belief system on the people. The power is in the mountains and the

Earth herself, in the stones and moon and sea. There is nowhere that it isn't!

This information on the Andean spiritual path is meant to be an introduction. It is perhaps over-simplified. Truth is something to be experienced, not so much defined in an intellectual way. This path is very much an experiential path, trusting one's own experiences within the world. It is meant to connect us more fully to the world in which we live.

Becoming a Comadre/Godmother

The role of a *compadre*, or literally co-parent, as so many things in Peru, is a bit more fluid than it is in other cultures. You are being invited to become a family member and it is a relationship which results in a strong lifelong bond. In its truest form, being a *compadre* becomes as strong a bond as the relationship between natural siblings or between parents and their children. In the Q'ero tradition, it means that they have chosen you because they view you as being pure of heart and as someone who will bring positive things and good luck to the family. There is no greater honor than to be asked to be a *compadre*. The female equivalent to this is a *comadre,* co-mother.

There is an overlapping of the indigenous practices with Catholicism amongst the people in Peru. Juan and his wife, Rebeca, consider themselves to be Catholic, but from what I have seen, their Inka traditions come first, and they squeeze in the Catholic rituals when it is convenient or necessary. The term *godparent* in most Latin cultures means that a person will help insure that the child is raised in the Catholic faith. There are a number of other ritual occasions which may include sponsorship of other Catholic sacraments (first communion, confirmation, and marriage) or sponsorship of a *quinceañera* (a girl's 15th birthday) celebration.

I certainly didn't qualify for that role. At that stage I had never even been to a Catholic mass and surely didn't understand the rituals. In order for a child to get into school, the godparent must sign certain documents, and if the child doesn't have a godparent to sign, the child cannot get into some schools. It appeared to me there were two levels to this relationship. The purely practical one of navigating through a predominantly Catholic society, and also the personal level, where one can truly become a member of the family.

There is a tendency in Cusco to ask foreigners to become *compadres* to the family, which baffled me for some time. I learned that this is for two reasons. Foreigners are seen as having more prosperity than native Peruvians, which has obvious benefits. Secondly, living in the same community as others requires more complex relationships which can be more challenging and can sometimes break down since there are so many levels to navigate within the relationship. I was told that by having the singular relationship with the *compadre,* it reduced the risk of that happening.

When asked to be a *compadre,* responsible-minded Westerners usually ask just what kind of responsibilities they are signing up for. In typical Peruvian style, they are told that there really aren't any, but underneath there is the hope that you will step up and do something to bring prosperity and a better life to the family.

Unlike in the U.S., a child usually has several *compadres.* My guess would be that they are not putting all their eggs in one basket, and they are hoping someone will pan out well. Foreigners leave, people move or die, and so many things are not reliable in Peru, that this actually makes a lot of sense.

In Peru, the person or people who do the child's first haircut ceremony become the *compadre(s).* When I was asked if I would come with Juan for his and Rebeca's third child's first haircut, I had two friends visiting Cusco, and they were also invited to assist me in this ceremony.

Juan and I set a time and place to meet. Juan and Rebeca, accompanied by their daughter, Yinifer, met us at the hotel where my friends were staying. Yinifer looked like a wild child. When they took off the gorgeous, brightly colored hat that her mother had woven for her, her hair looked as if it had never been brushed. It was matted and stuck out in every direction. Yinifer had just had her second birthday and was very shy.

We started out working with coca leaves, as in all of their indigenous ceremonies. We called in the spirit of Mama Coca, blew our *kawsay* into the leaves, and asked her to be present and to support us in the ceremony.

I was given a pair of dull scissors and asked to cut Yinifer's hair. I first cut out each little mat. I was to place the cut hair in a bowl and I was told that later they would bury the hair to give it back to Pachamama. My visiting friends also took turns in the cutting. Yinifer was very cooperative for a two year old who had strangers cutting off her hair!

We cut most of her hair, leaving her with a cute little pixie-style cut, but Juan and Rebeca wanted us to cut off *all* her hair.

I have always hated haircuts! To have to cut it *all* off was brutal for me! When we were finished, little Yinifer was exhausted and fell asleep. I saved one little lock of her hair for myself, and Juan bundled up the rest to take home and bury.

I felt that some sort of celebration was in order. I thought it would be really nice to go somewhere for lunch, perhaps somewhere they had never been. However, I was concerned about how well Rebeca's style of breast-feeding would be accepted in a nice restaurant. Breast-feeding is very common and well-accepted in Peru, but the women are usually just a little discreet. Rebeca would just leave one breast hanging out with no concern whatsoever about how that might be received by anyone else.

Added to my concern was that I was also aware of the discrimination against indigenous people by some Peruvians and I surely didn't want to put them in any kind of situation where our celebration could be compromised. I settled on a nice restaurant that I knew was owned by a foreigner. I thought he would likely be more tolerant and accepting.

As we were seated in the restaurant, I was successful at getting a table near a wall, and maneuvering Rebeca so that she was facing the wall so that when her breast was left hanging out, it would not be in view of all the people in the restaurant.

The Q'ero are "meat and potato" eaters. I also knew that Juan didn't like anything too spicy and that his favorite meat is chicken. There were two chicken dishes on the menu and one of them had *aji,* the popular Peruvian chili, so we opted for the other dish.

When it arrived, it had a beautiful presentation, which was chicken breast rolled with spinach and cheese, baked and sliced in a lovely spiral. The green of the spinach made a lovely pattern.

I will never forget the look on Juan's face when the dish was put in front of him. Q'ero cooking is pretty basic and plain, and there is always a huge quantity of food, quadruple what I normally care to eat. It astounds me how much they can eat! This was a couple of little spiral circles of the sliced chicken breast with side dishes in modest-sized servings.

Juan looked at me and said, "*That* is chicken?!" It certainly did not look like a chicken and there was not much of it.

In the future, I always let *them* choose the restaurant.

Journey to Q'eros
(What Was I Thinking?!?)

Juan and Rebeca got married in November 2011. Lesley and I, as godmothers to two of their children, were invited to the wedding in Ch'almachimpan'a, in the nation of Q'eros.

It is the custom of the Q'ero to live together prior to marriage, to make sure the couple is a good match. This is widely accepted as the sensible thing to do. At the end of a year or two, if it is determined that the couple is not a good match, they part, and there is no stigma at all attached to this. Marriage is seen as a conscious choice and a commitment for life. Children are seen as a natural outcome of a couple living together. If the pairing does not endure, the children are just absorbed into the family home. The Q'ero are extremely practical people. Without the use of birth control, it is not uncommon for one's mother to have children the same age as one's own—if you are the eldest, as Juan is. Juan and Rebeca had been living together for eight years before deciding to get married and had three children ranging in age from two to seven years old.

I was thrilled to be invited to their wedding in Q'eros. I was also scared silly. I had very limited experience with camping and cold weather, and I was about to embark on an adventure into both.

I was so glad that Lesley was going as well. She had been up there once before, so she knew what to expect. In truth, she wasn't so keen to be going again, which wasn't particularly reassuring, but I was ever-so-glad that she was!

She and her son, Simon, helped set me up with all the rental gear I needed for the four-day adventure. Juan had offered that we could stay in their house, but Lesley warned me that it was nothing more than a stone hut with alpaca skins thrown on the floor to sleep on. We would travel by van until the road ended, and then we would be on horseback for the next few days. The ceremony started in Chua Chua, the village Rebeca was from, where they would actually be married. Then we would move on to Ch'almachimpan'a, the village where Juan was from. They would eventually move on to Hatun Q'eros, the ceremonial center of Q'eros, but Lesley needed to return to Cusco before that. As I have mentioned before, the Inka fiestas last for days and days.

We went shopping for wedding gifts, little presents to give the children of the villages, and all of our food. We took all of our gear and goodies on a bus for three and a half hours from Cusco to Paurcartambo. We then took a van for another three hours to the end of the road. Narrow dirt roads, right on the edge of the cliffs the whole way—nothing even resembling guardrails! At least I didn't see all those little shrines by the side of the road like I have seen in other countries, in memory of those who went over the edge. Lesley assured me they were there, but I was not looking. I was thinking, *Well, there are worse ways to die. If I die, at least I died happy, doing what I want to do!* I was really not feeling fear, but every now and then I just had to look the other way when we got really near the edge of the cliff! (Lesley told me the road was new, and a real improvement since the last time she had come it was three days on horseback to get there.)

We waited at the end of the road for the horses and *arrieros* (horsemen) to show up. While waiting, we exchanged coca leaf kintus with the Q'eros that were accompanying us (they call this *halpie,* and it is a necessary bonding ceremony prior to any event), and they took turns playing a flute. The weather was fine, and for that I was grateful. It rains and mists a lot at the altitude of 15,400 feet—three miles above sea level!

I was feeling light-headed from the thin air, excited, and apprehensive. When they arrived, the horses had saddles, but no bridles or stirrups. *Yikes,* I thought, *This should be interesting!* We were assured that bridles and stirrups would be with the horses the next day (stirrups came, proper bridles never did). Our horsemen brought the horses, which were loaded with 2 or 3 skinned and beheaded sheep carcasses (on their way to the market, no doubt), relieved them of their loads, and reloaded them with living beings–us!

It was a bit of a challenge directing the horses with no bridle or stirrups, but apparently that is what the *arrieros* are for, they actually lead the horse, thank God! Luckily, they were good, well-behaved horses, didn't do anything too weird and pretty much just followed the path to the village. I couldn't complain, everyone else was on foot, only Les and I were on horses. Juan was carrying a huge sheet cake for his wedding *and* leading my horse at times.

Okay, Lisa, just go with it. And remember to breathe…

It was only a couple of hours to the village and I was happy that we had started early enough to arrive in daylight. Lesley was right, it was indeed a windowless stone hut. There were odd implements hanging from the ceiling–nothing I could readily identify. When I stood up, I had to dodge whatever was hanging from the ceiling, which of course, I couldn't see because there was no light or electricity, so it was dark inside.

It was the arrieros' job to look after us. My arriero was named Bonifacio, and he was 16 years old. They had the best attitudes one could possibly imagine, willing to do anything within their abilities. They started a fire in the alpaca/llama dung-burning stove which was made of adobe and was in the corner of the hut, to start boiling water to make us some tea and fill our hot-water bottles. My feet were freezing. We were way above the tree line, so there was no firewood unless they descended in search of it, so they burned animal dung for cooking. The room was soon filled with acrid smoke which burned my eyes. Lesley and I started arranging our sleeping mats and bags and doing all we could to get organized before night set in.

Getting organized was a bit of challenge, and we were racing against nightfall. We were trying to get the alpaca skins sorted out. I was imagining lovely, fluffy, furry skins, but these were stiff and lumpy, some with clumps of mud here and there, some with a bit of bone still attached to the skin. We were apparently in the storage house. It was stacked with bags of potatoes, some of which had spilled out and were sprouting, their little sprouts heading for the door which was the only source of light. We would lie on the skins to see if they were even, only to find random lumps which on further inspection turned out to be potatoes that had escaped their bags.

I decided to use my upturned hat for a nightstand so that I could put my hands on whatever I needed in the dark of night. Flashlight: check. Lip balm: check. Earplugs: check. Water bottle, oxygen can: check!

With no electricity, you really must learn to work around the availability of daylight. This was a new experience for me.

We were invited by the Q'ero women into what they called the kitchen, in another stone house, to cook our food. We had brought a cornucopia of vegetables and fruits to share. Silly me, I was imagining someone would be cooking for us.

It was pitch black inside, and the ladies were wearing headlamps which made cones of light through the thick smoke that filled the room. There were no windows in this hut either. There was no furniture at all, only bags of potatoes and the odd bucket which, if not in use, one could turn upside down to sit on. We had to work around the heads of the sheep whose carcasses we had seen earlier in transit, which were on the floor. The women invited us to cook first, which was most appreciated. The fuel used for the fire was mostly dried alpaca dung/pellets, with some dried horse manure and a couple of small pieces of firewood. It was surprisingly efficient. It was lovely and warm in there. It was very cold everywhere else! While we were eating, the ladies cooked potatoes for themselves, and were preparing the entrails of sheep, spreading them out on the dirt floor. Rebeca's mother and sister were there as well as Juan's sister, Julia. Julia had a baby alpaca with which she was making a stew for the celebration dinner the next day. Its skinless head was protruding out of the top of the pot and looked a bit like ET-in-a-pot. Just a bit creepy.

After dinner, we headed back to our cold hut and settled in for the night.

I have to admit, I was pretty freaked out–mainly about the cold and the sleeping arrangements. I had very little experience with sleeping bags and had no experience with mummy-style, thermal sleeping bags which really restrict movement. I felt like a little grub worm in that thing, squirming and inching my way around! Eventually, Lesley told me that the idea with the thermal sleeping bag is not to turn over inside of it, but to take the whole thing with you when you turn. That helped significantly.

My hot water bottle went cold pretty quickly. At that altitude water boils at 180°F, much lower than sea level. I had brought an alpaca wool hat with ear flaps, which was a life-saver for my ears! The air coming into my nostrils was so cold that I had to create a little tent to recirculate the warm air from my nose to stop my nostrils freezing. But then there was no oxygen in that air!

The floor of the hut was at a slight slant, and I kept rolling over onto Lesley. So, breathlessly, we created a bit of a wall between us using our duffel bags to create a barrier.

I was feeling more than a little bit claustrophobic, and it was so incredibly dark–I kept thinking "*WHAT am I going to do? I can't DO this! It is FREEZING! Who the heck am I to be here doing this? I have no experience with this–have I lost my mind?!??*" I had to take three Xanax to finally get to sleep. I had a -15 degree sleeping bag and a lovely warm and soft inner sheet, but I couldn't get the zippers in the right places, and as I squirmed about, they kept coming unzipped, and the frigid air came rushing in. With the increase in altitude, it was exhausting just to try to rearrange the sleeping bag and I was huffing and puffing every time I turned over! And the floor was also on enough of an incline that I slid down and completely off my sleeping mat in my sleeping bag a couple of times during the night and I would wake up freezing. The ground was very cold!

And the DARK! I kept finding excuses to turn on my flashlight just to reassure myself I hadn't gone blind! Lesley and I finally had to have a good laugh at how ridiculous it was to hear to each other struggle in the dark and then take a moment to huff and puff and catch our breath–there is so little oxygen at that altitude!

Well, I did eventually sleep okay–better living through chemistry–and thank God for Xanax!!

The next morning we woke up at around 8:00, and Bonifacio warmed up the leftovers from the night before for breakfast. I really wasn't very hungry, probably because of the altitude. Les and I were fetched to come to a prenuptial meeting (attendance was required of the godparents) where it was discussed what was expected of the couple in the marriage. It took place in another stone building with a grass roof and no windows. Juan & Rebeca were in their wedding clothes and were very quiet and reverent. Instructions were read from a book, mostly in Quechua so I couldn't understand, but I peeked at the book and there were some drawings as well. They kept passing around a qero (a drinking vessel) of various drinks which we were required to partake in, and I started feeling a bit tipsy. Those drinks apparently had alcohol in them, and at that high altitude, it doesn't take much to start to feel it. I was thinking *I probably shouldn't really be sharing germs with everyone in the room,* but I really didn't have a choice. I would come to regret that a few hours later.

After that, we went to the ceremonial area where the wedding party sat at a table at the back of a tarp-covered area, and various people came by to greet the couple. I saw the wedding party get up to leave, and I remembered that we were supposed to accompany them, though I had no idea where to, and I also had no idea where Lesley was. I followed the small party up a hill, and we ended up in the school building at Chua Chua, which is where the wedding was to take place. Eventually, the whole village meandered in, including Lesley. I had saved a seat for her next to me in the front row.

As people came in, they laid offerings on a plastic sheet which had been laid out in the front of the room. Some were liquids in plastic bottles, many were small quantities of earth wrapped in paper or plastic. The wedding party sat in the middle of the front row of chairs, quiet and stoic, with their heads bowed while everyone filed in. They looked so beautiful and noble, and I felt blessed and honored to be invited into their world for a few days. Yinifer, their youngest child (my goddaughter) played at their feet with a metal cup.

Eventually the wedding was officiated. It sounded to me like the service was in Quechua sprinkled with some Spanish words. I couldn't understand what was being said. The rings were kept in a bowl covered with a cloth, carefully guarded by a man who was sitting to my right, who I later found out to be Benito Machacca Apaza, the President of Hatun Q'ero and Juan's godfather. He is a lovely man and has a gorgeous, happy face, full of character.

Apparently, there was a requirement that the wedding couple was to stay in a deep inner space of meditation and contemplation prior to, throughout and for three days after the wedding. The couple is never to leave each other's side, and is flanked by various relatives, officials and godparents. They are each tied to the person flanking them by a ceremonial ribbon. (Needless to say, there is no "honeymoon"–they already have three children!) They are surrounded by people who are celebrating, but they are required to keep their heads bowed, be demure and not converse or partake in the celebrating (though I did see a few beers sneak in after a couple of days). Yinifer was mostly at their feet during the days of celebration, under the table in many cases, and I did see her under Rebeca's sweater in the church helping herself to a snack at Rebeca's breast.

Immediately following the wedding, there was the baptism of two children, and Lesley had been asked to be godmother to them both for the baptism. It looked to me like a spontaneous decision–kind of like, "Well, everyone is here and now we have a godmother. Let's do it!" One of the children was Juan's brother, Luis's youngest daughter, named Lydia and the other was Juan and Luis's youngest brother who was 4 years old, named Segundo.

After the wedding and baptism, everyone went back to the ceremonial area and started partying. They got drunk fairly quickly. Although there is no electricity in Q'eros, someone had rigged up a car battery to a boom box and had mounted loudspeakers on one of the grass rooftops and the Peruvian music started! It was aimed directly at the house where we were staying, and it never stopped the rest of the time we were there. It played all day and all night for days and days. It was surreal to be in a village that hadn't changed a thing in the past 500 years, but had modern Peruvian music belting its way through the mountains! The beat permanently embedded itself in my brain. (When I got home first thing I did was put something ELSE on to stop the repetitive beat going on in my head!)

I was starting to get concerned about the time, since it was supposed to be two or three hours by horse to the next stop at Ch'almachimpan'a and it had been dark by 6:00 the day before. So Lesley and I packed up our things, rounded up Bonifacio, and headed out–the wedding party didn't plan to leave until 11 p.m.

These people have powers that we don't have!! They really can see in the dark, stay upright on slippery muddy slopes in sandals and still have warm toes, thrive on potatoes and alpaca and navigate a horse over a mountain in the middle of a frigid, black night! I couldn't imagine riding a horse through these mountains in the dark while being drunk!! I was really glad we left when we did.

We arrived safely at Ch'almachimpan'a, but it was a fairly harrowing ride through some very rocky terrain and slippery shale. I would never have wanted to do it later, I'd have been terrified! The path was very rocky, foggy, with shear-edged cliff drop offs. The descent was very steep, and I had a hard time staying on my horse, even with a saddle.

Lesley and I set up our bedding in Juan's house–very similar to the previous one, stone walls, thatch roof, no windows, dirt floors and sacks of potatoes–and we went to bed very early–

around 7 p.m. My main goal was to be in a warm place, and my sleeping bag appeared to be the only option. My feet were blocks of ice.

Note to self: Two pairs of normal socks DO NOT equal one good pair of thermal socks! Buy thermal socks.

I was definitely getting better at the bedding, but Bonifacio had thrown the skins on the ground in such a way that we were on an incline again, and I kept sliding down the mat. Still, I was surprised at how well I slept. And I was equally surprised that I was able to go to the bathroom outside, squatting against the side of the house, with my bare ass out in the cold. Actually, I was out there pretty frequently. It was apparently not a great idea to share a drinking vessel with the entire wedding party. They are accustomed to all kinds of bacteria that we are not. I finally had the brilliant idea to cover my frequent "deposits" out there with a stone, to avoid stepping in them on my next visits.

First thing in the morning, we peered out our front door, and it was snowing!! It stuck to the mountains in the distance, but melted the moment it hit the ground where we were. Still, it was very, very cold!! It snowed for a couple of hours. I was wearing wooly leggings, jeans, water/wind proof rubber-backed outer pants, two long-sleeved thermal t-shirts, two alpaca sweaters, my jacket with its heavy lining, two pairs of socks, thick leather boots, an alpaca Peruvian hat along with my sun hat. I had even let the hair on my legs grow out in hopes of staying warm! Still my toes were numb most of the time. Les and I each looked about twice our size! Most of the children there were barefoot, and the adults wore only their traditional sandals, and their feet were not cold! This Florida girl just finds that hard to fathom! Okay, so the good news is–there are virtually NO insects up there. No small wonder....

That day was the all day party at Ch'almachimpan'a. It was really more of the same thing that had been going on at Chua Chua, just with a new venue. The ceremonial area had been decorated with yellow and white balloons, gorgeous, colorful streamers and confetti, and all of the paraphernalia, drinking vessels, chicha (corn beer), and beer, had been moved from Chua Chua to Ch'almachimpan'a.

We went to greet the newlyweds, and had to wade through many drunken Q'ero who were all dancing and staggering around in the snowflakes. The dancing, celebration, and drinking went on all day.

Juan and Rebeca stayed introspective and contemplative for the three days that I was with them, even at times when the ceremonial table was virtually toppling over, due to various drunken men who were dancing and staggering all around them.

I was having a very hard time staying warm. My feet felt like solid ice blocks. Every chance I got, I went back to my sleeping bag with a hot water bottle to try to get warm. I wandered around the small village taking photos of the stone houses in the clouds and popping in and out of the ceremonial area. I did notice that the women were not drinking, but tending to the various men, many of whom were passed out right on the bench where they had been sitting or on the cold ground, propped up against a wall or pole.

I slept quite well that night! I finally got the zippers of my sleeping gear sorted out. After much discussion and prodding, Bonifacio took care of the incline problem with our bedding by adding more skins to the bottom of our sleeping pallet. We had given away most of our food, thinking that we were contributing to the main meal. We never did see that food again, mostly vegetables (which don't grow at that elevation so are considered a real prize and may have been interpreted to be a gift), but at midday we had been handed a plate with a mountain of alpaca, noodles, potatoes and rice–most of which I couldn't finish. So for dinner we just warmed up what was left in our food supply, which was all fruit, and made compote which we shared with Juan and Rebeca.

Lesley had made plans to leave the next day since she had to be back in Cusco for several reasons. I was supposed to go to Hatun Q'ero with the wedding party for the final celebration destination over four hours away by horse, but I was really quite ready to get back to a warm place. I was tired of dodging drunken men, tired of trying not to drink too much liquid so that I didn't have to pee in the night or at an inconvenient time, and tired of looking for things in the pitch black in our hut. My camera was going through batteries like crazy at that high altitude/cold temperature, and I had to take two more Imodium due to the fact that Bonifacio was tearing up dried horse manure for the fire with the same hands that were preparing our tea and meals. All water had to be fetched from the one spigot over the hill, and though Bonifacio was an absolute dream in terms of his attitude and willingness to do anything at all to please us, he was only 16 years old and had limited experience in the world and obviously, with good hygiene.

I must say though, what a charming young man he was. He wanted to make everything right, though a few times we had to get fairly firm with him on what he considered acceptable or "*Nor-mal*", as he kept saying. He'd get this high pitch to his voice sometimes, especially when he said "Si!" that was so cute and engaging!

That night at 12:30, the door to our stone house swung open and a number of people came in with flashlights, set up bedding and went to sleep. It didn't faze me one iota (thanks again to the drugs!) In the morning, I found a young man, a woman with two tiny children bundled up and sleeping on top of a sack (which I nearly sat on top of, thinking it was a stack of rags), two other women by a fire they had built, and perhaps there was someone else, but I couldn't see in the dark, even in the morning, especially with the smoke from the fire. Many of the people had battery operated head lamps strapped to their heads that they used to see in the dark. The light from the headlamps reflected off the smoke in the room. I could see my breath and also the steam rising from whatever was cooking and the cups of tea or coffee.

I looked down and one of Lesley's boots was creating a small cloud that was adding to the fog. "Les, why is your boot smoking?" I asked. "Oh, I think I dripped some water on it." she replied. The whole thing struck me as very funny, and I went into a fit of hysterical laughter, which was much needed at that stage! Even when there was light, you still couldn't see across the room indoors! Yeah, I was definitely ready to get back to civilization!

We had made arrangements to get up early to head out for our return trip to Cusco. I finished the last of my granola bars for breakfast and we packed up and headed out to look for the horses.

We were told that before we were allowed to leave we had to go dance at the celebration area. They were all still there, Juan and Rebeca, on their fourth day of holding space quietly, tied by their ceremonial ribbons, surrounded by jovial drunken men dancing, playing flutes and drums and professing their love of the world. They are such happy people!! I only saw one time when someone who looked like he'd had too much to drink might have been getting out-of-hand, and he was quickly subdued by two other men and a woman who kept tugging on his ears, for what reason I had no idea!

We finally were able to break away from the fiesta-thon and get to our horses. Lesley had the same, even-tempered horse all the time, but I got whatever horse they could find and the one they had readied for me clearly did not want a passenger. I very nearly got kicked when trying to mount. They had told me to be careful of him, he was *Maldito* (Cursed One).

Lesley had no stirrups and I had no bridle or horseman. Luis was supposed to come with us, but we couldn't pull him away from the party. I went to try to retrieve him but I could see he was starting to get a little bit "happy" again.

I threw a bit of a hissy fit, insisting that I have a bridle and calmer horse, that I did not want to die, and I could not possibly manage a horse without a bridle. Especially based on the last two experiences when the horse decided to go another way whenever he wanted and wouldn't stay on the path!

So instead, the cargo was loaded onto Maldito, I eventually got a rope for a bridle and a calmer horse, Lesley got a saddle with stirrups and Luis did eventually join us. There was another couple who had planned to ride with us, but they never turned up, and it appeared that there weren't any more horses anyway, so off we went. ("Welcome to Peru!" as everyone was always saying in such instances!) Luis and Bonifacio were on foot and Les and I and our luggage were on three horses.

The weather was beautiful! I did still have on two long sleeved t-shirts, two sweaters and my jacket with lining, insulated gloves, wooly leggings, jeans and water-proof pants, two pairs of socks, boots (my toes were still completely numb from the cold!) and two hats (in truth, I never changed clothes the whole time I was there!) but it wasn't raining or snowing. It misted quite a bit, and rained lightly a few times so I was very glad to have the water-proof pants. The sun peeked out a few times and the three and a half hour ride went very smoothly.

Luis danced up on the ridge, then got way ahead of us and laid down on the rocks to nap while we caught up by foot on one of the steeper descents where we had to get off the horses.

As huge as that valley was that we were riding through, you could see right across it, and Bonifacio pointed out to me that way off in the distance there was some movement, and there was our other horseman on his way to Ch'almachimpan'a with another four horses, probably for the other guests to ride back. None of the horses were tied–they were all just running along with him down the side of the canyon. It was so beautiful to see and felt like something from another era.

During the last hour, Bonifacio took the lead for my horse, and we just went quietly through the valley. It was such a beautiful ride. The mountains were dotted with many white alpaca, and I got to see some birds I had never seen before and also some Andean geese.

Bonifacio was very patient in helping me with the proper Quechua pronunciation of the names of the birds, stopping and turning around so I could see his mouth and mimic his sounds, but of course, I forgot it all within minutes anyway.

We passed the skeleton of a horse on the ground and a small cemetery with makeshift crosses on the graves. We got into a tiny village called Anccasi, around noon. There was no restaurant, but a man opened a little dried goods store, and we were able to buy crackers, tuna, and sodas. We said good-bye to Bonifacio. Our combi (van) had been arranged for 1:30, but at 2:00 the three other waiting passengers were saying that it wasn't coming. That's another Peruvian custom I was adjusting to. They just say things as if they are fact, regardless of whether it has any basis in truth or reality. I have always been such a literal person and take such care to be as responsible and accurate as possible in the things I say, so this comes as a bit of an adjustment for me. So I learn to not believe anything until I see it for myself.

I was really not looking forward to another night of camping. There were no hostels or restaurants, and we had no tents. The owner of the shop had closed up, and we were sitting on a pile of eucalyptus logs, getting drizzled on, napping and praying that the combi would come. We eventually convinced the shop owner to open up and let us take shelter in his shop again as it had gotten very windy and cold. At 2:30 the combi finally arrived to take us to Ocongate, to catch the bus to Cusco.

We were crammed into the combi, I got a window seat, and Luis hopped in beside me. Luis dozed throughout the trip (Luis has the sleeping-while-sitting-up thing down pat!) and two hours later we arrived in Ocongate. It was so nice to walk on my own two feet after hours and hours on horses and buses! We bought our bus tickets to Cusco and Les and I found a *polleria* (rotisserie chicken place) and bought three dinners to go which we took back to Luis and ate on the bus. It was a lovely, luxury bus and wasn't very full, for once! We spread out, and I watched the scenery until it got dark, then I tried to nap like everyone else. My seat was directly under the speakers, and I was pummeled into a pulp for the next three hours by the same Peruvian music that we had in the village for the last three days and nights. It occurred to me that this could be a new form of torture–nonstop blaring music day and night, I was desperate for some peace and quiet!!

Surrender, Lisa! Just give it up....And for heaven's sake, buy an MP3 player in the very near future so you can at least have some choice in music when taking public transportation.

I could not believe the state of my fingernails! They had never been so dirty in all my life! I had not seen running water in days and days (heck–I had not seen my fingernails in days since it was always dark indoors, and whenever I wasn't indoors, I had on my gloves!) Though I picked at them for hours while riding on the buses, I had to bleach them once I got home to get them clean!

We got into Cusco after dark and Les and I shared a taxi home. I always love coming into Cusco, but that night it was absolutely heavenly to see Cusco's twinkling lights come over the horizon, looking like a starry night sky as they climb up the sides of the mountains!

****

Going to Q'eros fulfilled one of my life's dreams. All of my life I have said that if I could have just one wish granted, it would be that I could become invisible at will. I could board any plane and fly anywhere I wanted. I could come and go in and out of places and see how people live and interact. I have been blessed in my life to have a lot of opportunity to travel, but I always felt that my presence inhibited people from behaving as they normally would. The cultural anthropologist in me finds every aspect of humanity fascinating.

I did get to be invisible there amongst the descendants of the Inka. Me being there didn't change a single thing. And I got to witness another world, up in the clouds at Q'eros.

Q'oyllurit'i - The Snow Star Festival

The Q'oyllurit'i Festival happens during the end of May/beginning of June each year. It is a pilgrimage to the Sinakara Valley and the glacier at 15-16,000 feet above sea level, made by the faithful in reverence to their beliefs.

Juan had been encouraging me to go to Q'oyllurit'i for years. After my experience in Q'eros, I really had no desire to go camping at high altitudes with no services again. I trust Juan implicitly, but there is just no way a 16th century, robust, healthy young man is going to have any clue what my needs are as a middle-aged, coddled 21st century gringa in an extremely foreign environment, living in a tent at below freezing temperatures.

Once Lesley and I arrived up in Q'eros for Juan and Rebeca's wedding, we never got to interact with Juan again personally for the entire time we were there. In fairness, it was his wedding, so he was otherwise-engaged, but we were really left to our own devices to feed ourselves and stay warm. Q'oyllurit'i would be no different since Juan is an *ukuku* ("bear" in Quechua), a ceremonial dancer and part of the policing body of the festival. He had his own responsibilities and family to take care of and didn't need me to tend to as well.

The first couple of years my answer was a flat out "no" in regards to making the pilgrimage to Q'oyllurit'i, but Juan is a patient man. He was gently insistent. He felt it was a very necessary step in my spiritual path. And then I saw an "in."

I had a friend named Seti Gershberg who had been in and out of Peru for a few years, making a documentary on Peruvian shamanism. We shared many interests, and our paths kept crossing until we became good friends. His documentary was focusing partly on the Q'ero, and partly on the jungle shamanism surrounding Ayahuasca.

192

Seti invited me to come to Q'oyllurit'i with him. Seti, being an American who also organizes tours to Peru, would totally understand my needs and offered to help keep me comfortable. He arranged all the gear and food. Seti had become very close with the Q'ero family that he was spotlighting in his film, Don Humberto and Doña Bernadina Sonqqo and two of their sons, Guillermo and Rolando. I had worked with all of them in the past.

Guillermo was going to accompany us, along with his wife, Marcosa and two of their children, Roxanna, who was about eight years old, and their baby boy, Mika, who was four months old. I felt safe going with them. On Saturday, May 26th, 2012 we headed out for our four day adventure.

****

The Q'oyllurit'i Festival predates the Spanish conquest and has been celebrated for hundreds, if not thousands, of years. It coincides with the full moon and is in celebration of the return of the Pleiades/Seven Sisters constellation over the horizon, which disappears from view in April in the Southern Hemisphere and signified a time of chaos for the people. They would look to the constellation to assist them in knowing when to plant and harvest. It represents a time of transition from old to new, the upcoming harvest and Inti Raymi–the Winter Solstice (the biggest indigenous festival of the year in Peru) which is celebrated a few weeks later.

Of course, the Catholic church has always been very good at incorporating existing festivals and important dates of the lands that they pursued into their local repertoire, and Q'oyllurit'i is no exception. There is a story about a miracle that occurred in this valley in 1780 involving two young shepherds and an image of Christ that appeared on a big rock. A shrine has been built around the rock and the image of Christ, which they call the Lord of Q'oyllurit'i, that the Catholics come to visit. Annually, as many as 70,000 pilgrims come to this festival to show their

193

dedication to their faith throughout the four days of the festival. There are very heavy Catholic overtones by all these people dressed in their native clothes!

Many of the people of Peru have an interesting combination of indigenous beliefs and Catholicism. The 10-20% of Peruvians that survived the Spanish Conquest in the 1500's only did so by moving their belief systems underground and hidden in the Catholic imagery, as happened in many other countries. Over the centuries it has become more ingrained, and now, instead of parading Inkan mummies through the streets, they parade Catholic saints. This was a very necessary survival tactic. In my view, reverence is reverence, and I don't see it as hypocritical or unacceptable to see these belief systems overlapping the way they do, though many tourists are baffled by it. Many people are surprised to find that the Q'ero consider themselves to be Catholic. Again, they are very practical people. They do what they must to survive, and they do what works. The Inka had a reputation for being flexible in their belief systems, and they also incorporated the best of whatever culture they were dominating (which was one of their keys to success), so this was not a new concept for them.

Nowadays, people from this region make the trip by bus to the town of Mawayani, at the foot of Ausangate, the second highest peak in Peru (just under 21,000 feet above sea level) and considered to be the most sacred *apu* (mountain spirit) to the Inkas. From there, they make the eight and a half kilometer trek on foot (or horseback in my case) at 15,000 feet above sea level to the Sinakara Valley where the festival is held.

There are many ornately costumed dance troupes here, dancing in honor of their devotion. There are also humble peasants with loads on their backs which symbolize the burdens that they carry in life. Most of all, there is reverence. The air is infused with marvelously intense veneration and devotion, whether it be indigenous or Catholic. It is a magnificent sight to behold!

194

Once we arrived in Mawayani, we went to go find lunch and Guillermo organized horses for us to transport me and our cargo of tents, food, gas bottles, etc. Once the horses were loaded, we started the five-plus mile trek to our destination. The ride was surprisingly easy, and the dirt road was quite level. There were many pilgrims traveling with us, and many coming back from the other direction as some people make it a day trip.

There were several crosses along the way that had elaborate drapes of cloth over them, and some of the faithful would stop at each cross and say prayers. There were enterprising individuals all along the way that had set up cooking stands and they sold drinks and edible goods along the way.

My horseman, or more appropriately horse*boy*, looked to be 9 or 10 years old. He was not very good at not running into other people that were coming from the other direction. I don't know why it is (keeping in mind that I grew up in the flat-as-a-pancake state of Florida) that in Peru the horses always want to walk right along the edge of every precipice and mountain, but they do. My attitude of *"if I die, at least I died happy"* has taken me a long way in these circumstances. Yikes, this was not a trip for people with vertigo! Luckily, the horse was a smooth ride and very well-behaved.

After an hour, I wanted to get off the horse and walk for a bit since my knees were killing me. Silly me, I dismounted to the left, as always, which was not the mountain side of the road, but the sheer cliff side. What I did not expect was for my knees to buckle as my feet hit the ground. In order to not fall off the edge of the cliff, I frantically grabbed for the saddle and ripped the top half of one of my fingernails off. Ouch! That really hurt! Though it probably didn't hurt as much as falling off the cliff would have…

We arrived in the valley just after dark and set up our tents. This time I had rented a down jacket and not one, but two sleeping mats and sleeping bags. I had learned that I just move around too much at night for those mummy-style sleeping bags. I zipped the two sleeping bags together, and I had a huge double sleeping bag with a double wide inflatable sleeping mat! Seti had gotten me a three-person tent so there was plenty of room for all my stuff. I was definitely getting better at this!

Seti and Guillermo set up the dining tent, and we had dinner and an early night. I couldn't believe I was at Q'oyllurit'i!

****

The next morning there were ice crystals on the outside of my tent. I had brought a thermometer with me and it was 30°F inside my tent. I slept in my two sleeping bags, down jacket, alpaca wool hat and thermal socks and I was nice and warm. I was feeling quite pleased with myself.

The real festivities were not to happen until the next day, but we were glad that we got there a day early because the whole valley was filling up fast! By mid-day, people were getting downright territorial about space, and we ended up spending many hours arguing over space. There were people coming in who maintained that we were in their designated spot. We had to call over officials, who said we were okay, but these people were really persistent! We ended up having to take down and move our tents over a bit twice, and we had to remove one tent altogether to appease them. Most of the tents were eventually butting right up to one another, and to get anywhere you had to dodge everyone's tent lines. It ended up there were only a few paths to get in and out of the tent city. Having to take down one of the tents meant someone had to sleep in the kitchen tent, which didn't have a covered floor and the ground was cold. Seti volunteered to take it, but Guillermo insisted that his family would stay there, saying that it was a much bigger tent for the four of them and that they were accustomed to the cold. I was looking at their beautiful four month old baby and thinking "*It is awfully cold to have such a young baby here, but what the heck do I know?*" They insisted that they would be just fine.

The squabbling over space was starting to feel a bit hostile to me and certainly no longer reverent. I didn't even feel safe leaving my stuff there without someone there to guard it, and it appeared that that someone was going to be me. Seti and Guillermo went up the mountain and I stayed back, and it is a good thing I did. I ended up having to fend off these guys who were so insistent that we had to move, and I had become very stubborn. We had moved our tents over twice and taken one down, and I just kept saying "No! I am not moving again!" Besides, there was nowhere to move to, since by then every square inch was already occupied! It was really a fairly miserable day, and I had lost my sense of wonder and beauty. This was not feeling spiritual at all.

That evening, after Guillermo and Seti came back, some people that we knew stopped by for a visit, and we cooked and ate dinner. Guillermo found someone to guard our tents, and we were granted permission to visit the Q'ero section of the area, which was up the hill next to a huge black boulder.

Once I got up in with the Q'ero, even though I didn't see anyone I knew, I felt so much better, I felt at home! The difference in energy was palpable. I was introduced to lots of people, but it was so dark that I couldn't see anyone's faces so I had no idea whom I had met. Then I saw that Juan's brother, Luis, was there, so there was a familiar face, but he was practicing his ceremonial dances for the next day. I just watched and soaked in the love that I was feeling and breathed a deep sigh of relief. *This was why I was here!*

The mountains surrounding that valley are so high that the sun is only visible in the sky from about 9:00 a.m. to 3:00 p.m. Of course it is light for a couple of hours either side of that, but the sun is only available for warmth during those six hours, and it starts to get colder at 3:00 p.m. By 6:00 p.m. when the sun has gone down, the temperature starts to plummet.

I was tucked up in my sleeping bag by 8:00 p.m. There was a roaring drone of music, talking and singing outside my tent, punctuated by the popping of fireworks every few minutes. Thank heaven for earplugs!

****

The next morning Juan and Rebeca had arrived with their baby, and Juan came down to see us. The moment I saw his face I knew everything was going to be fine.

What is it about that man that I love so much? I see him and every cell in my body just relaxes. His being is so sweet and so pure. My feeling for him is very familial, as if I have known him and known I could trust him forever.

Juan was dressed in his *ukuku* garb, a long robe-like thing of black fringe with a big red fringed cross at the front. When they dance, they also wear a knitted mask with holes for the eyes, nose, and mouth, with embroidered ears, eye lines and moustaches. He had a whip lassoed around his neck. The *ukukus* have to earn the right to be an *ukuku*, by being exemplary citizens and going up the glacier and surviving the cold. Mythologically speaking, they are considered to be the offspring of a woman and a bear and are feared and respected for their superhuman strength. The *ukukus* are also the policing body of the festival, and if anyone is acting disrespectfully, they are asked to change their behavior, and if they don't comply they will see that whip in action. The *ukukus* also use the whips with each other in a dance, in a show of machismo, whipping each other's ankles without showing any sign of fear or pain. Strangely, the *ukukus* also play the role of the trickster and speak in high-pitched voices when they are in costume.

My dear, sweet Juan with a whip around his neck—I couldn't imagine it! "Are you going to use that thing?" I asked.

"Yes, I am," he said, raising one eyebrow. The thought made me wince.

We went up to Q'ero-ville, as I called it, and everyone was readying themselves for the dances. I was beside myself with

198

excitement. I had my best camera in tow, and these were some photo opportunities that would be any photographer's dream come true!

All of the sudden, they just took off, dancing the whole way while moving at lightning speed, and we were scrambling to keep up with them. I kept running into people I knew who required the obligatory greetings, hugs and kisses, and then I would scurry to catch up and find them amongst the throng of people, all the while trying to not step in the numerous water channels that had been dug to channel off the snowmelt. I did not want wet shoes, socks and feet in that climate!

What a wonderful day we had! To watch the people that I love so much at the height of their cultural exhibition in dance after dance after dance!

Some were doing the dances of the *ukuku*. Rebeca's father was there doing the dance of the Wayri Ch'unchu, representative of the inhabitants of the jungle, with wooden staffs and feathered headdresses. They wear a tall crown of the long red feathers of the macaw, and draped down their backs are strands of smaller red and blue feathers and beads. What a gorgeous face that man has! So joyful and beautiful, sweet and kind!

Lots of the dancers are the Qhapaq Qoya that represent the small, indigenous Aymara population from the altiplano who were the legendary merchants. These dancers were wearing the same knitted mask as the *ukukus*, but different clothing. They wore a beautifully decorated square, flat-topped hat with gorgeous patterns of sequins and antique coins hanging around the rim. They have a small stuffed vicuña (the animal from which the domesticated alpaca descended) hanging off their backs. We were told the vicuña was there to absorb any *hucha* (heavy energies). They are usually also making the motion with their hands of twisting wool into thread.

After the dancing was over in the afternoon, Guillermo, Juan, Seti and I went up the mountain to do a *despacho* ceremony and a *karpay* (initiation) for Seti and me. This was the reason Juan wanted me to come to Q'oyllurit'i. This was another energetic transmission for us, bringing all of the lineage of the Q'ero to us.

The *despacho* ceremony was massive and beautiful. I felt so deeply grateful to be present and to be the recipient of this great honor by Guillermo and Juan. An initiation at the Q'oyllurit'i festival is a peak experience in this spiritual path. I was deeply humbled, and it was a crowning glory to a magnificent day and experience. Juan gifted me with a brightly colored Q'ero ceremonial hat, usually reserved for the men. My heart was so full I thought it would burst!

Yes, yes, yes. This is why I am in Peru! This makes my heart sing!

****

Early the next morning Seti and Guillermo went up the mountain to the glacier. I felt no need to do that–I had gotten exactly what I wanted already! I stayed with Marcosa down below and took amazing photos of her baby, little Mika, who was all wrapped up in colorful blankets with a woolen hat and his dear little face peeking out of the bundle. He had been coughing a bit and was a little cranky, but the photos came out great.

They said they thought they would be back down the mountain around 11 a.m. We figured it would take about eight hours to get back to Cusco, and that would have us back at a decent hour. While they were gone, I busied myself taking down and packing up my tent and belongings and socializing with friends that were stopping in for cups of tea. Guillermo had arranged for the horses and horsemen to be there at 11:00. I had seen the horsemen in the morning, but 11:00 came and went, 12:00 came and went, and when Seti and Guillermo finally returned the horsemen and horses had left!! I guess they got a better offer!

Though I was feeling very happy, I was ready to go home and sleep in my bed. My back was aching and my toes were cold. Juan and Rebeca had already left to go back to Q'eros. It was looking like we might be spending another night in that cold valley. About 80% of the people had already left, and it barely resembled the amazing festive place it had been 12 hours earlier.

Guillermo ran off to Q'ero-ville to try to do damage control. He came back with two cousins and three horses that had been headed to Q'eros but agreed to help us out. We were most grateful to be heading back to Cusco, trailing behind the crowd.

My horse ride back was kind of comical. This horse wanted to *go!* He kept whinnying when we stopped for any reason. As long as he was moving he was okay, not quite as smooth a ride as my horse coming in, but I was the only person in sight on a horse at all, and I was still glowing with the joy of the previous day. I was also feeling very happy to have accomplished something I never thought I would accomplish.

When we finally reached Mawayani three hours later, Seti was trying to round up all of Humberto's family, but it was a bit like trying to herd chickens. I just sat back and watched. We had lost Guillermo's cousins and the pack horses carrying our gear shortly into the trip. We had stopped at the half way point and waited for them for some time, but they hadn't turned up. For all we knew, they were ahead of us. I wasn't as concerned about our belongings disappearing as I might have been if our stuff wasn't with Guillermo's relatives. We eventually went off to get some dinner in one of the restaurant tents and waited for things to settle down a bit. It was such bedlam there with everyone trying to get out of town, and all our people wandering off in every direction. It was starting to look like we may have to pitch those tents again. *Ugh! I wanna go home!*

Eventually our guys and gear turned up. I had stopped looking at the time and wondering how long we were waiting for things to come together. In Peru things either happen or they don't, and the sooner one surrenders to this the less frustration one is going to feel. We spent quite a bit of time trying to negotiate our way onto a bus, but demand and prices were high. Finally, we found a nice public bus, and when I got on I was pleasantly surprised to see that Luis and his family were already on it. Seti was running around trying to round up the Sonqqo family. In the end, I think we took off without Bernadina, but that was the best we could do. She knew how to make her own way back to Cusco.

It was nearly midnight before I got to bed. I was filthy, and I really didn't care. I was getting in that bed! I slept like a baby, I was so grateful to be home once again! I was so pleased to have made that journey and to do so much better than I did on my trip to Q'eros the previous year! I thought *I am really not the person I used to be. I am really happy!*

****

Two days later I got a phone call from Seti telling me that little baby Mika had died. We were both absolutely stunned and shocked.

What!? That beautiful little baby that I took so many gorgeous photos of two days ago?! How is that possible?! In my world babies don't die!

We were not in my world. We were in the world of the indigenous people of Peru, the world where they have no health care. The world where a baby dies from a cough. The world where half of the babies never make it to their first birthday. Mika died. Guillermo and Marcosa took his little body up to Q'eros. They have lost four of their eight children.

Well, you can imagine my dismay! In speaking to my friends that are familiar with the ways and customs of the indigenous people, their response was, "Q'oyllurit'i always takes a few."

I went straight down to the photo shop and had those photos of Mika printed and enlarged and I framed the best one. They were such beautiful photos! When we got word that Guillermo and Marcosa were back in Cusco and staying with his parents, Seti and I went up to Don Humberto and Doña Bernadina's house south of Cusco and we gave the photos to Marcosa. She

202

cried. We all cried. She had never had a photo of the children she had lost before, and she was so grateful.

Yes, life is a fleeting gift.

Hatun Karpay - Grand Initiation

Hatun in Quechua means "great" or "grand." *Karpay* in Quechua technically means "irrigation" and it is the word they use for "initiation." This is a ceremony which is performed once you have been on the Andean spiritual path for long enough, once you have received the prerequisite initiations, and once you have proven that you are serious about your work on the path. It takes you into a deeper level of energetic transmission.

In the Andes, the way that you become more involved with and show your commitment to the Andean spiritual path is a combination of "right living," doing ceremonies–frequently *despacho* ceremonies, to honor and connect with *Pachamama* and the *apus*, and also by visiting the sacred mountains themselves.

When you visit the *apus,* you go with your teacher or someone who is willing to share his/her lineage with you. You start by doing a *despacho* ceremony on the mountain to ask for blessings and permission to work with the *apu.* If all goes well, you are then given an energetic transmission called a *karpay.* Then you are offered a *khuya,* a sacred stone, from that *apu* which becomes a part of your *mesa*, the sacred bundle that you work with on a daily basis in meditation that connects you directly to that *apu* when you are not there physically.

Usually, your first few karpays are to germinate the seed of the path that is within you. If you would like to become a *pampamisayoq*, which is in essence an Andean priest, you need someone who is already a *pampamisayoq* to be willing to give you the energetic transmission. There are a minimum of three *karpays* required over a period of time to become a *pampamisayoq.*

As much as I love working with the Q'ero, their teaching style is very indirect and takes a very long time. You work side-by-side with them for 20 years, and you slowly take it all in by osmosis. When given the opportunity, I have always taken advantage of supplementing my learning from other Westerners who have put in the years of work and can teach me in English, and in a learning style that is more familiar to me.

Elizabeth B. Jenkins started on the Andean spiritual path more than 20 years before I did and has written an excellent book called *The Return of the Inka* about her experiences. Her teacher is Juan Nuñez del Prado, a native Peruvian who was a professor of Anthropology at the University at Cusco and whose teachers were a Q'ero Master named Don Andres Espinoza and another Peruvian Cusco Master named Don Benito Qoriwaman. Juan's father, Oscar Nuñez del Prado, was a leader in an expedition which rediscovered the Q'ero in 1955 and identified them through their weavings as the direct descendants of the Inka.

Elizabeth offers a ten day *hatun karpay* each year in Peru. It is a deep immersion in Inka practices at their sacred sites, and I was given the opportunity to join one of her groups in October of 2012, which I eagerly accepted.

They follow a very specific prophesy which requires that you go to numerous sacred sites around the Sacred Valley and Machu Picchu for various *karpay* ceremonies. At the end of the teachings and initiations of the *hatun karpay*, you are offered the *karpay* initiation which they refer to as "The Fourth Level" *teqse paqo* or *initiate*.

It is a beautiful path with wonderful teachings, and it is basically meant to move you to a place where you are operating out of a motivation of love in everything you do. (I personally feel that it shares a similar goal with many other spiritual paths, the one with which I am most familiar is *A Course in Miracles*.)

I truly felt that doing this work with Elizabeth in my own language and in a learning style that resonated with me took me to a new level of understanding. I highly recommend it for anyone who is serious about deepening their experience on the Andean spiritual path.

As Elizabeth says on her website at www.thefourthlevel.org, "The Hatun Karpay Initiation is a conversation with Nature in her most powerful state, within the sacred Inka geography….is spiritually arduous, [and] physically rugged…" It is not for the faint of heart, and it is extremely powerful!

Moving into the 21ˢᵗ Century

How did I end up with the job of helping a man and some of his people make the leap from the 16ᵗʰ century to the 21ˢᵗ century in a few short years? I am not altogether sure how it happened, but it was my honor. This was my mission, and it brought (and continues to bring) so much joy and meaning to my life.

Peru is a fascinating country. It is so incredibly rich with history and diversity. And it is so poor–it has suffered through much domination, oppression, and corruption. It is a country of contrasts and offers numerous learning opportunities to try to understand the depth of the culture and society. There are many marvelous charities that want to make a difference in the world, and a lot of them end up in Peru. Peru is abundant with opportunity to be of service.

Health care and education are not free in Peru. I saw charities that sponsor doctors to come and offer medical care to people that may otherwise die without it, in the outlying communities. There was one charity that went out into the villages daily to teach the preschoolers Spanish, so that they could enter school. They brought toothbrushes, taught them basic hygiene, and gave them nutritious snacks to give their young brains something to work with besides potatoes.

There were charities that helped the women get organized into weaving guilds so that they could offer their magnificent weavings for sale. Other charities taught the villagers skills that they could use to better their lives and support themselves, like building greenhouses so that the *campesinos* could grow vegetables in the colder climate.

There is so much beauty in these generous acts. They can also be double-edged swords that have implications that are difficult to anticipate.

I found myself involved with a few different charities whose intentions were to assist in the transition process, to help the Q'ero who wanted to come into the 21st century to do so, and hopefully preserve their cultural identity. At the time, it seemed like an answer to my prayers–the opportunity to be of service.

We can step into things with the best of intentions, with stars in our eyes, believing we will be "helping," and being a bridge between these two worlds.

Making this transition while preserving the beauty and integrity of their culture in the face of technology and wealth proved to be far more complicated than we ever imagined. There were so many aspects of human nature that came into play which we could not have foreseen.

Improving the quality of the water in Q'eros doubled the population in quite a short time, and the land could not support so many people. This was less of a problem because many of the Q'ero started moving to the cities, in hopes of better lives and education for their children

The children must speak Spanish to go to school in the city, which they learn quickly, but it alienates them from their parents. The men learn some Spanish, but the women stay at home and don't have the opportunity to learn it. Programs were set up to teach the women Spanish, which had limited success.

When a young man is sent off for further education and he returns with a laptop and smart phone, he is no longer living in the same world his parents do. To maintain the level of respect between generations that had endured for centuries in this traditional culture is difficult for an educated child whose parents are illiterate. The transition is not a smooth one.

When people live in harsh and challenging conditions, they frequently must work very closely together to survive. If a man is sick and can't plant his fields, his neighbors and family will come to help. Otherwise, his family will die of starvation in the coming year.

With abundance, plenty and excess, greed can seep in. From what I have seen, greed and envy are almost like infections that can come in if one is not mindful, or if one has not been taught how to manage them.

I have spoken with many people who have voiced a frustration with working in the various charities in Peru. Sometimes they discovered that the results of the work they came to Peru to do with the best intentions, was not having the impact they thought it would have. When you are dealing with a disempowered group of people who have been oppressed for so long, where any inclination towards innovation has been completely squashed, you may have thought that what you were doing was giving them a "leg up," a boost which, once in place, would allow them to take off, and help them to make things happen on their own.

Without understanding the cultural impact of their history, these loving people are disappointed to sometimes find that Peru actually sees them as an ongoing source of income. It sometimes seems it actually inhibits the government from putting programs into place that would be more sustainable and beneficial for its impoverished citizens. They are very happy to take hand-outs on an on-going basis.

So we do the best we can. My key goal throughout the process of helping the Q'ero that I worked with was to "teach them how to fish," rather than just giving the "fish" to them. Integrity is my absolute bottom line. If we can't do it with integrity, then we aren't going to do it at all.

The Q'ero are highly discriminated against by the dominant Hispanic culture in Peru. That is, until they need a shaman. When they want the best shaman around, they look for a Q'ero.

Part of it is the nature of man to need someone to look down upon to elevate their own status and egos. Part of it is the influence of the self-serving superiority that organized religion has encouraged. In truth, the minimalist lifestyle and hygiene of the indigenous people offends the modern societies that choose not to look more deeply into another's culture to see what beauty may be behind it.

Juan finds himself between a rock and a hard place. The mainstream society has a "who-do-you-think-you-are?" attitude to anyone who aspires to elevate themselves beyond what their society thinks is "their place" in their imagined hierarchy.

Juan's people are traditionalists. This is why this ancient civilization has endured for 500 years and why the Q'ero have the reputation of having the most pure ancient Inka traditions and practices. Juan is even judged by his own people for wanting to grow and change and *envidia*, (envy) or jealousy also comes into play.

Juan finds it hard to find someone who will celebrate his achievements with him. I am his cheering committee, and I love my job! There are people that try to change the world in a big way. I have always known that that was not my path. But I have the honor to help a few individuals change their world, and in my opinion, this does change the world.

I must say, it is far more complex than we ever imagined. Human nature is fascinating and not always pretty. I know that this goes on all over the world in other societies that are making this transition from more primitive societies into the modern world.

My little corner of the world is one of many. We do the best we can…with integrity.

****

There is also much beauty that can be seen in this process, and plenty of opportunity for a good laugh. Here are a few of my favorite little anecdotal stories that I feel really shed a bit of light on some of the interesting challenges:

Juan and I met one morning to do some emails. We had been working for an hour and a half when I turned to him said, "I'm hungry. Are you hungry?"

Juan said. "Si, Comadre, I'm starving." The Q'ero are always hungry. It amazes me the quantity of food they can consume, and I have to take this into account when I feed them.

I said, "I have eggs, would you like some eggs?"

"Si, Comadre, I would love to have some eggs."

"How many eggs would you like, Juan?"

Juan looked at me and blinked. He looked at the ceiling, he looked at the floor. He looked at me again and blinked.

"How many eggs does a person normally eat?"

No one had ever asked Juan how many eggs he wanted. He didn't know. There are chickens in Q'eros. But I guess when they have an egg, they eat it.

****

Juan and his wife, Rebeca, came to my apartment one morning. I knew Juan was coming, but I didn't know Rebeca would be with him. In an attempt to be a good hostess I made some toast. Even bread is a treat for the Q'ero. Wheat doesn't grow at their high altitude, so they don't have wheat flour to make bread.

There is a magnificent jam in Peru called *sauco*. I had never seen it in the United States. It looks a little bit like small blueberries in jam, but it is more red than purple. It was super yummy and not particularly cheap, but I had treated myself to a rather large jar.

Juan and Rebeca sat with their little plates of toast and the large jar of jam on the table. They mounded their toast with as much sauco as could possibly fit—it was dripping down the sides. Knowing that they are not accustomed to our rules of etiquette, I tried not to show the surprise on my face when I saw their toast heaped with my expensive sauco jam. Sweets are hard to come by up in Q'eros.

Note to self: *In the future, NEVER put the jar of jam on the table when the Q'ero come to visit.*

****

Juan was at my house and I decided to make some popcorn. All I had was the microwaveable popcorn, so I put it in the microwave and set the timer. As it started to pop, Juan looked at me with a panicked expression on his face and said to me, "Comadre, what is that noise?"

I told him, "Juan its okay. Look!" Then I took the bag of popcorn out of the microwave and I opened it and poured it into a bowl. The look of relief on his face was priceless. For me, it was one of those defining moments. I just wanted to hug him and teach him all that I could to help him make the 500 year jump through the ages with grace and integrity.

****

I was doing my grocery shopping and it occurred to me that since I was going to meet Juan at noon, why not have him meet me at the grocery store and help me carry my groceries home? Since I don't have a car I can only really buy what I can carry. I am limited to shopping pretty much once a week. I don't really like shopping very much and given the opportunity I would prefer to shop for the whole month while I am at it. It occurred to me that I do so much to help Juan, it would seem reasonable for me to occasionally ask for his help when I need it.

The Q'ero are so unassuming, so sweet, so grateful—Juan would never dream of questioning my purchases or even looking into my bags. He dutifully helped me carry them from the taxi up the stairs and into the kitchen. I had bought a lot of produce, and

I thought this might be a good opportunity for a lesson in "how to keep gringos healthy" since we had planned to take a group up to Q'eros soon. I was trying to teach him as much as possible to ensure that our group participants stayed healthy. I decided to teach him some of the secrets that I'd learned about how to stay healthy in Peru with limited hygiene.

I opened the cabinet door under my kitchen sink, and I brought out a bottle of Clorox. I asked Juan, "Do you know what this is?" Well, of course he would always like to be able to say that he knows, but we've gotten close enough now that he just looked at me and hesitated and then said, "Clorox. No, Comadre, I don't know what that is."

I explained to him what Clorox is. I said, "This is poison. If you drink it, you will die." Juan's eyebrows shot up, and he looked at me with some concern. I then said, "If you spill this on your clothes it will make a hole in the cloth."

Some form of recognition came across Juan's face, and he said, "Oh! I knew a guy that used that on his hair once and his hair fell out!"

I said, "Exactly! This is serious stuff. But if you use it in very small quantities, it can be very helpful. The problem with gringos staying healthy in Peru is that our systems are not accustomed to some of the bacteria here. Watch this."

I filled up the kitchen sink with cool water and then very carefully put two drops of Clorox in the water. I carefully placed all of the fruits and vegetables in, explaining to Juan that certain vegetables are guiltier than others of making gringos sick–for example, green leafy vegetables, like lettuce, spinach, basil and cilantro–and green onions. I told him that because we sometimes eat them raw, they are frequently the culprits of harboring the bacteria that make us sick. I told him that the bacteria hide in all the little spaces and crevices so it's very important with those vegetables that they be very, very clean.

"It isn't really necessary to put in bananas, avocados, and cucumbers because we don't eat the skins, but I do it anyway just to be sure. This is because when you touch the vegetable that

212

hasn't been cleaned and then you touch the other vegetables, the bacteria can go from your fingers onto the food. I really don't want my friends to get sick from food they've eaten at my house, so I just put everything in this water, and then I can just relax and know that the food is safe. I generally leave the fruit and vegetables in this water for fifteen minutes, and then I rinse them off with regular water here at home. But if we are out in the country and we're using mountain water, the mountain water has bacteria in it too, because the alpacas and llamas and sheep poop in this water sometimes. It isn't a good idea to rinse it with mountain water. A tiny bit of Clorox is okay to consume. A lot of Clorox is not good to consume, but a little Clorox is better than bacteria that are going to make them sick."

Juan took this all in and found it all absolutely fascinating. He was very diligent about making sure that the fruits and vegetables were out of the sink after fifteen minutes, then rinsed each one with tap water and put them in the drainer.

"And this is how we keep gringos healthy!"

****

Trying to explain the concept of sea level to someone who lives at 15,400 feet above sea level and has never seen the sea is a bit of a challenge. But Juan is very smart, so I explained the physics of how water boils at a certain temperature at sea level, and by boiling the water, it kills most of the bacteria.

I then explained that as elevation rises, the air pressure changes, and water boils at a lower and lower temperature. So we have to boil the water for longer in hopes of killing the offending bacteria. Water boils at 212°F at sea level, but in Q'eros it boils at 180°F, hence our past problem.

****

I had been talking to Juan for months about bacteria and parasites and the problems they cause gringos. Juan was always eager to learn and he was a great student. But one doesn't know what one doesn't know.

One day it dawned on me that Juan was not getting the whole picture. He was very willing to accommodate, but he didn't really understand what I was talking about.

"Juan, do you know what bacteria are?" I asked.

A look of "uh-oh" came across his face, that odd space between wanting to know and not wanting to admit that he doesn't know.

"Mmmm….no," he confessed.

"These bacteria are so tiny that you cannot see them, Juan. They are so dangerous that they can kill."

I then pulled up some videos online to teach him about bacteria. I left him alone to watch them in the living room, and I just got on with what I was doing in the kitchen. Every now and then I would glance over at Juan. His eyes were open wide, staring at what he was seeing in the videos and the looks of consternation combined with disgust on his face were priceless.

It was a challenge not to laugh…

Return to Q'eros - Wamanlipa

Juan had been gently nudging me for years to go back to Q'eros to do a *despacho* ceremony at the Q'eros' most sacred *apu*, Wamanlipa. One evening, he gifted me a *khuya,* a sacred stone, from Wamanlipa and it blew me away. I just sat there for hours, clutching the small stone in my hand, repeating, "Wamanlipa. I have a stone from Wamanlipa. Wow!" I felt the stone's energy penetrating my hand as I held it; its power seeping into me, traveling up my arm and becoming one with me.

Q'eros seemed so far away. Though this was clearly a key part in my spiritual path, I really had no desire to make the arduous and frightening trip up there again. My first journey there had been so incredibly uncomfortable. On my later trip to Q'oyllurit'i, I had certainly gotten better at learning how to stay warm and what sort of gear I needed to survive in the harsh conditions, but I still got sick, and it took quite a while to recover once I got back to civilization.

I found that in the Andean spiritual path the *apus* came to me in various ways. Mostly, I just found myself en route to one of them to do a *despacho* ceremony, either by invitation from someone else or something I felt called to do myself. I have found that things are never laid out in front of me with explanations as to what I need to do and why. In my daily meditation, I always ask for guidance and support in what is best for my soul's highest and best purpose. Sometimes in my meditation I am given a very simple instruction, and I choose to believe that this is an answer to my prayers. Ever since I have detached from the "hows and whys" of things, my path has unfolded in ways which are much more fulfilling.

Apu Ausangate is considered the most sacred *apu* in the tradition. The energy of this powerful mountain, at an elevation of nearly 21,000 feet, feels masculine and authoritarian. He always struck me as incredibly imposing, but I hadn't really connected with him one-on-one. When Ingrid and I first came to Cusco and rented the third floor apartment which I would live in for the next few years, I was most surprised one day to look out my bedroom window to the south and see Apu Ausangate staring back at me from 40 miles away. He is frequently shrouded in clouds so I hadn't noticed before. It was kind of like being a child playing in the attic and suddenly you see your father's feet in the midst of your game. It was as if I would look up to see he had been standing there for some time, watching me.

OK, I got the message….

I had been to Apu Pachetusan for one of my initiations, and Q'oyllurit'i for another one, two other power spots. One time, when I was returning to Cusco in an airplane, I had closed my window shade because the sun was so bright. I felt a very strong energetic pull coming from outside my window, so I raised the shade to see what it could possibly be.

Wham! There was Apu Salkantay, massive and white, covered in snow, just outside my window! Salkantay is the second most sacred *apu* in the Andean spiritual tradition and the third highest peak in Peru, just after Ausangate (and Huascaran, in northern Peru). Salkantay translates to *Savage Mountain* and it certainly feels it. To be so close to this magnificent mountain, which is not really very easy to access from the ground, felt like an energetic jolt and a blessing to me! Ausangate is at the far southern end of the span of mountains that the Andean spiritual tradition holds as most sacred, and Salkantay is at the far northern end. They stand as sentinels and massive power points.

One day I was having a coca leaf reading by Amado. Earlier in the week I had an unusual energetic experience which had sent me to bed for 24 hours–I had been unable to function that day with what I was feeling. I couldn't tell what it was, I had never had that particular experience before. I asked Amado if he would ask the coca leaves for some clarity.

Amado called in the spirit of Mama Coca, and we both blew on the leaves, putting our *kawsay,* our life force energy, onto them. He held a handful of leaves about a foot above the table

216

and let them slowly fall from his hand onto a cloth he had positioned on the tabletop. He looked at the way the leaves had fallen, put his hands on his thighs and nodded his head while pursing his lips and humming "Mmmmm-hmmm." I waited in anticipation for his interpretation.

"What is it?"

Amado took a deep breath and blinked a few times, still staring at the leaves. "Mmmm-hmmm", he hummed again. He looked at the leaves and said, "It was an *apu*."

"An *apu*?!" That was the last thing I was thinking it would be. I had been helping to facilitate a number of plant medicine ceremonies with groups in the previous month. The energetic experience didn't feel exactly familiar, but I guessed it had more to do with the plant medicine ceremonies than with *apus*.

"Which *apu* was it? Pachetusan?"

I couldn't help but assume it was an *apu* that I already had an established relationship with. Pachetusan always felt very nurturing, and it was significant to me since it was where my first initiation had taken place. Or perhaps it was Wakay Willka/Veronica, a very powerful *ñusta* (feminine *apu*) where I had received my first *khuya,* in the shape of a heart.

"No, this is from a major *apu*."

Apprehension came over me. To be honest, these more powerful *apus* actually frightened me. Once you connect with them directly, they can be very demanding and unwavering in their expectations of you. You are in service to them in helping them accomplish whatever it is they are doing.

"Uh-oh….." I closed my eyes and took a deep breath, bracing myself.

"There is a message here for you. It says:

Lisa, I am waiting for you. —Salkantay."

I gasped. I heard myself say in a tiny, incredulous voice, "Salkantay?"

"Yes, Lisa. You have just received a *chaska,* an *estrella*–a star, I believe you call it in English. This is when an *apu* calls you to come to it. You have to go to Salkantay. You had taken on too much *hucha,* too much heavy energy, during those plant medicine ceremonies. Salkantay has chosen you and cleared the energy for you."

I felt like someone had hit me over the head. I felt stunned, dazed, frightened and a bit baffled. *I thought I was being of service, and I did all I could to pull in protection during those plant medicine ceremonies. How am I going to get to Salkantay?? I am not a trekker–I am a wimp when it comes to this physical stuff! Yikes! Salkantay??*

I spent a couple of months trying to work out a way to get to Salkantay. Eventually, I just surrendered to it and, as usual, a path to Salkantay made itself available to me.

I was at a social function and the man sitting next to me worked for a company that organized specialized lodge-to-lodge treks on the magnificently beautiful five day trek from Salkantay to Machu Picchu. This company used the hotel where I worked on a regular basis for their trekkers during the time that they were in Cusco. I knew the owners of the tour company because they stayed at our hotel from time to time.

He worked it out that we could get a ride with the tour company van on a day when they were taking their trekkers on the 3-hour drive from Cusco to the first lodge. We could spend the night at one of their gorgeous lodges, complete with meals, so we wouldn't have to camp outdoors. We could get up early the next day for our journey to Salkantay.

Juan had a Q'ero friend there who was in charge of *despacho* ceremonies for the tour company. He would arrange horses for us to get up the mountain. We could come back with the van from the tour company in the evening.

It took six months for all of this to work itself out. Roger had come to Cusco for another visit and he, Juan and I all went together. It was an amazingly beautiful experience. We took the horses up as high as they could go. When the horses could no longer navigate the slippery shale at the pass, we went the rest of the way up the mountain on foot, climbing over the huge boulders along the way. I felt held by Salkantay, I was never afraid. These mountains will actually feed you energy if you ask for it. I was totally energized!

At the pass, we did our *despacho* ceremony to honor Salkantay, to give thanks for our safe passage in our journey to get there, and to ask for permission and blessings in the ceremony we were about to perform. We did our initiation work. Then, with our hearts full of the energies of Salkantay, we made our descent back down the mountain and back to Cusco.

****

There was going to be no such shortcut to get to Wamanlipa. It would take a full day to get to Q'eros, even with the new roads. We would be walking or traveling on horses from where the road ended. There were certainly no luxurious lodges to stay in, just stone huts. I had learned during my trip to Q'oyllurit'i that a tent is actually warmer than the drafty stone buildings. Plus, no one would be burning animal dung inside my tent, whose acrid smoke I would have to breathe throughout the night along with the thin air. I could have a tent to myself and have my privacy without people coming in and out throughout the day and night.

It had been two years since I had gone to Salkantay and Q'oyllurit'i. Wamanlipa had been working its way into my heart, I could feel it. It didn't feel demanding in the way Salkantay had felt. More like a patient parent who is just waiting for you to come home when you are ready.

In the summer of 2014 I met a lovely woman named Danni. She was Australian and, like so many of us, had come to Peru on what she thought was to be a short stay, and then couldn't bring herself to leave. She had connected with Juan and she also loved to dance to the same music I did. Over the next few months, we went out dancing together in Cusco, and our friendship deepened. We looked at one another one day and realized that our paths were dove-tailing. Juan had invited her to Q'eros, and she felt the call deeply. We went back up to Pachetusan together to do a ceremony and initiations with Juan, and shortly thereafter Danni became godmother to one of Juan's children. We had become family.

I found Danni very easy to be around. She had the ability to go into incredibly deep, intense experiences with an attitude of deep gratitude and simultaneously a lightness-of-being that somehow enhanced things. She laughed so easily; it was a pleasure to be in her company. One day I told her that I was considering going back to Q'eros, and I was trying to feel out what would be the best way for me to do it. I knew of many people that wanted to go to Q'eros, but I did not want the responsibility of looking after other people in such challenging circumstances. This was feeling like it was going to be a very personal journey for me. I didn't want to be required to split my attention and take care of people who would likely be sick at that altitude with the rustic conditions.

Danni, in her typical, easy-going manner said, "Okay, let's sit with it and see what happens."

Much to my surprise, we soon set a date with Juan to go to Q'eros in the following November. My main goal was to go to Wamanlipa, in line with my spiritual path, as Juan had been encouraging me to do.

However, Juan and I had a group coming the next year that had been with us in Peru a couple of years before. This group was deeply dedicated to the Andean spiritual path and wanted to go to Q'eros. I had not been to Q'eros in three years. The group that was coming also wanted to go to places in Q'eros that I had not yet visited. It was starting to look like I needed to do a trial run of the route. It was all coming together.

Danni and I were both nervous about making the trip. In my previous adventures of this kind, someone else had been in charge of supplies and making arrangements. This was falling on us to do for ourselves, and we were having to trust in Juan, who is much more hardy than either of us. But we both felt supported by each other. I felt good having Danni for company—she wouldn't put heavy demands on me. Danni felt good coming with me because I had been there before, and my Spanish was better than hers.

I also wanted to take this opportunity to teach Juan more about the kinds of things that gringos need on a trip like this—what they need to be comfortable and stay healthy. The altitude alone is cause enough for many people to have a difficult time. The lack of good hygiene in these high mountains with the only water source coming from the runoff and snowmelt that are shared with the animals, is a sure bet that there will be problems if they are not addressed properly.

The day came, and just the three of us, Juan, Danni and I, made the trip to Q'eros. We were met by Juan's father, Mateus, on the way and when we arrived at the town of Chua Chua (as the road had made its way further into Q'eros in the three years since I had been there) Juan's uncle, Mariano also joined us and stayed for a couple of days.

Juan's brother-in-law, Jose, also joined us the following morning and accompanied us for the rest of the time we were there. Things went incredibly smoothly until the end of the third day when we arrived in Juan's village of Ch'almachimpan'a, at an elevation of 15,400 feet above sea level. The weather had been marvelous in spite of the fact that we were entering rainy season. The horses were great and we'd gotten really good camping gear. We'd brought our own water, since it was only Danni and me that needed it, so I'd even managed not to get sick.

We had been on the horses for 4 or 5 hours to make our way from Hatun Q'eros, with a picnic lunch break along the way. When we arrived at Ch'almachimpan'a and had set our tent up, Danni looked at me and said, "I think I'm about to go down." And down she went in our tent, the altitude had gotten to her. The next day was supposed to be the highlight of our trip, our first visit to Wamanlipa, the most sacred *apu* in Q'eros. I had been trying to get there for years!

We kept Danni in the tent, occasionally using the can of oxygen we'd brought, and supplying her with water and light food for the rest of the day and night. I was really concerned that we were not going to be able to go to Wamanlipa to do our *despacho* and *karpay* the next morning.

But the next morning Danni felt much better, and she felt that she was up to ascending another 1,600 feet to do our ceremonies at 17,000 feet above sea level in the shadow of Wamanlipa.

We left early to start the hour and a half journey by horse up to Wamanlipa. We passed herds of alpacas and sheep on the ride, and we rode the horses until their hooves could no longer keep a grip. We made the rest of the climb up on foot.

When we got to the top, Juan looked over to what looked to be solid clouds and informed us that Wamanlipa was there, behind the clouds. I must say, I was terribly disappointed that we wouldn't be able to see the mountain, even though we knew it was there. Before we'd left Cusco, we had done a *despacho* ceremony to ask for safe passage on our journey, and that everything go well. I couldn't believe that after all this time of trying to get back to Q'eros, here we finally were and we were going to have to settle for just knowing that the most sacred mountain on the Q'eros' spiritual path was deep into that wall of clouds.

Just then, as if it was a curtain, the wall of clouds parted in the middle and moved to either side, exposing snow-covered Wamanlipa in all its glory! I was moved to tears! The curtain of clouds stayed open for about 10 minutes, just long enough for us to see Wamanlipa and take a few photos, and then it closed again.

We were so grateful!! It felt as if that spectacle had been orchestrated just for us! Afterward, we did our *despacho* ceremony and *karpays* in the deepest of gratitude.

During the energetic transmission that Juan gave me, I felt the crown of my head open up. Juan had opened my poq'po, my energy bubble, so that I could receive the sacred light of his lineage. Just at that moment, the sun came out and I felt bathed in glorious light. I thought how fitting it was that the sun should shine on me in that particular moment. I opened my eyes, and the sun was not out at all, the wall of clouds had completely enveloped us. The light I was feeling was not from the sun, it was the light of Juan's lineage shining during our *karpay!* Danni and I both felt as if we had been filled with the magnificent pure *sami* energies, as if we were actually in the *hanaq pacha*, the upper world! It was truly a prayer answered and a dream come true!

****

Back in Cusco, feeling so thankful and accomplished that I had finally achieved a return trip to Q'eros, overcoming all of my fears and apprehension for my inexperience, I genuinely felt that I had reached a new level, a deeper level on my spiritual path. I felt relief that it was behind me now and pride that, in spite of my inexperience and age, that I had fulfilled this dream of mine.

Another dream of mine was fulfilled as a result of my trip to Wamanlipa. For years and years I have been a storyteller. I would tell my stories and people had always said to me, "Lisa, you should write a book! You should share your stories!" I had even started to write one a couple of times, but I was always completely frustrated in the process, to the point of giving up. My father had written a couple of books, so it seemed as if maybe one day I could do it too.

One day after my return to Cusco, I woke up and I realized that a book was coming together in my head. It happened so quickly! Every day new chapters were coming to me, how they were to be organized and all I had to do was to take the time to get them out of my head and onto paper!

I do not profess to be any more capable than the next person. If anything, I have always been considered to be less than average when it comes to anything requiring physical strength or fitness.

However, I was blessed to be born into a family that believed that you are capable of just about anything that you set your mind to. You just have to be willing to take that first step. I am so appreciative of the opportunities that have been given to me!

This much I know is true: what I have learned was that what I really needed was faith. I needed to learn to trust the world and myself. I needed to let go of what society had told me would make me happy and listen to my own inner guidance, and follow it. I learned that there is something much greater than me, and if I tapped into that energy, and rode on the wings of faith, that doves could fly in my heart.

References

Plant Spirit Medicines
Ayahuasca & Wachuma

There has been an increasing interest in the use of visionary plant spirit medicines globally in recent years. They have come to be known as *entheogens* which translates to "generating the divinity within." They are also referred to as psychoactive substances and people who learn to navigate the worlds that can open up to them using these master plants, sometimes call themselves "psychonauts."

The following information is meant to be a brief introduction, and a resource and reference guide for where you can find out more about them.

****

Wachuma / San Pedro Cactus (*Trichocereus pachanoi*)

The San Pedro cactus grows in the dry highlands of northern Peru. The "Wachuma Cult" is first documented near the areas of Huaraz and Chavin de Huantar, and has been documented as having been in use for over 3,000 years.

This plant is legal in the U.S. as a garden plant and can be bought in many plant nurseries or online. The plants that are used for ceremonial purposes are usually a minimum of seven or eight years old and have been grown in a very dry climate, which is what makes the concentration of the active ingredient (mescaline [3,4,5-trimethoxyphenethylamine]) strong enough to create its effect. There is a gray area around the legality of having this plant in your possession. The body of the cactus only becomes illegal when you prepare it for consumption.

The entire plant is not consumed. There are parts of the plant that are very purgative, and usually those parts are cut out when preparing the body of the cactus for consumption. The spines, outer waxy skin and inner core are cut away. The pulpy, inner part of the cactus is cooked into a brew or dried and made into a powder.

As a plant spirit, Wachuma is considered by most to be a much more gentle spirit than Ayahuasca.

****

Ayahuasca (*Banisteriopsis caapi* & *Psychotria viridis*)

Ayahuasca is a vine that is native to the Amazon jungle. To be effective, it must be combined with another plant, usually Chakruna. It is possible to brew it with the addition of other plants, but using just these two plants is considered by many to be the most pure.

If you were to consume either of these plants alone, nothing would happen. The chakruna has DMT (dimethyltryptamine–one of the most powerful hallucinogens in the world) in it which causes hallucinatory visions, but this is normally digested by the acids in the stomach if eaten alone. The Ayahuasca vine has MAOIs (monoamine oxidase inhibitors) in it, and only when combined do they become the brew that is used ceremonially as Ayahuasca, or *Yagé* as it is called by the indigenous people who have used it for centuries.

The energies of this plant spirit are extremely powerful. You really must have an experienced shaman with you to help manage them. You will be very spiritually vulnerable, and more harm than good can be done if you do not have someone who is experienced at managing these energetic forces and has a good relationship with the spirit of Ayahuasca.

****

Living in Peru, where access to these plant medicines is legal and easy, has given me a different perspective on them. In countries where they are illegal, the mainstream mindset is that they must be illegal because they are dangerous, and many people assume that they are addictive. It is also the inclination of Western thinking to break these magnificent sentient beings down in to their various chemical parts and talk about them as if they are predictable pharmaceutical drugs.

Nothing could be further from the truth.

My experience in working with these plant spirits is that they are healers that you can call upon to help you with emotional, physical and spiritual healing. The spirit of the plant may or may not choose to work with you. There is no guarantee that you will get what you are asking for. There is no guarantee that you will get anything at all. Your attitude going into this work has a lot to do with the outcome.

I am not talking about the "if-you-believe-it-it-will-work" sort of thinking, though that too can have an effect. I am talking about respect and reverence. Just like when you are working with a human being or an animal, if you show respect, you are far more likely to develop a good relationship.

There are many people who approach imbibing these plants as just another opportunity to get high. Sometimes that does work, and sometimes it doesn't. Sometimes there are people who go into the experience with the right attitude and the plant spirit still decides not to work with them. We usually don't find out exactly why, but we trust the intelligence that has made that choice. Sometimes the plant spirit will give you the exact experience or information you need to heal, and sometimes it will give you a healing that you need before you are ready to heal the wounds which you are actively seeking to heal. Sometimes the experience points you in a direction of where you need to go to start your healing process and sometimes the plant will even send you to work with another plant spirit.

I have even seen instances where another plant spirit will enter a ceremony and block the effects of the plant spirit that a person thought they were going to work with. In this case, it was the spirit of cannabis. The plant spirit of cannabis came in and informed the shaman that it was blocking the effects of Ayahuasca to certain people. Not everyone who smoked cannabis was blocked. The block was made because these people had given their personal power away to cannabis, and had an addiction to it.

I know there are many people who don't agree that cannabis can be addictive. I make this statement based on the admission by some of the people involved that they were, indeed, addicted to it. It is possible to become addicted to anything. It really depends on the individual and their attitude. If you have given your personal power away to something, it can be addictive for you.

I would like to add a few words of caution to working with these plant spirit medicines. First of all, they are illegal in most countries. That in and of itself is a major issue. But more importantly, if you choose to investigate this further, please come to it with respect and reverence. Do some soul-searching, inner work and research. Use your intuition to help you know if this is a good path for you. I would recommend that you do it in a country where it is legal.

I would also advise that you allow yourself enough time to work with it properly. This is not a one afternoon experience and then you just get on with your life. There should be a preparation period for you to do your inner work, possibly limit your diet and exposure to other substances and/or drugs and sometimes a requirement to limit sexual activity. There is the day or night that you do the ceremony, and afterwards there should be an integration period. The following day, even if the obvious effects of the experience are finished, the plant is still in your body and it is still working on you.

I always recommend that the following day you have completely free with no plans. This integration period honors the work that you are doing and allows it to go deeper. I have had experiences where nothing happened until the third night when powerful prophetic dreams came to me. I have had experiences where it seemed nothing much was happening during the ceremony itself, but the weeks following brought such unlikely and powerful events into my life that I had no doubt that it was the plant spirit working with me, bringing to me the experiences that I needed. It can be quite baffling trying to figure out what is going on and why. It was only in retrospect that I was able to see that some of these experiences were for my personal benefit, and some of them were for the benefit of other people in my life, but that by having these events happen, it brought balance to our relationships in the long run. This is why they are referred to as Master Teacher Plants. I could never have orchestrated these events myself!

It is also suggested that you take the minimum dose of a plant medicine that you can. The first time you are doing this, you are likely to have some anxiety about it, it being a new and potentially life-changing event. That anxiety alone can have a very strong impact on your experience. Fear can completely dominate your mind and stop other valuable things from happening. So be gentle with yourself. Dedicate some time to this process. The first time take a low dose, see how it is going to feel. The second time you will have much less anxiety and things are likely to go more smoothly than if you launch off the first time into a high dosage experience.

Be sure that you have someone that you trust to help take care of you during and for the 24 hours after one of these experiences. Sometimes when people have had an intense experience they just want to be alone. And sometimes, especially if they are still feeling the effects, which in my experience can last up to 24 hours, the last thing in the world they want is to be left alone. You need someone who is sensitive and responsive to your needs. Sometimes you don't even know what you want, so an intuitive and sensitive person is helpful to just have someone to sit with you, and allow you your processes without interfering.

Unfortunately, with the increase in interest in these ceremonies and the rise in esoteric tourism, there has also been a problem with scammers and people claiming to be shamans who are not qualified to lead these ceremonies and can even be dangerous. When under the influence of these powerful plant medicines, you are very vulnerable. People have been robbed and sexually assaulted by these fraudulent people. Please be sure that you know who you are dealing with. Investigate the reputation of every individual and every retreat center before you open yourself up to these experiences.

There are some excellent resources online. Here are a few websites to get you started:

www.erowid.org

www.ayaadvisor.org

reset.me

www.realitysandwich.com

Here are some excellent books on Ayahuasca:

- Ayahuasca: The Visionary and Healing Powers of the Vine of the Soul by Joan Parisi Wilcox
- Breaking Open the Head: A Psychedelic Journey into the Heart of Contemporary Shamanism   by Daniel Pinchbeck
- DMT: The Spirit Molecule: A Doctor's Revolutionary Research into the Biology of Near–Death and Mystical Experiences by Rick Strassman
- The Cosmic Serpent: DNA and the Origins of Knowledge by Jeremy Narby
- Sacred Vine of Spirits: Ayahuasca   by Ralph Metzner Ph.D.

There are fewer books written on San Pedro/Wachuma. These are my favorites:

- The Hummingbird's Journey to God: Perspectives on San Pedro; the Cactus of Vision by Ross Heaven
- Cactus of Mystery: The Shamanic Powers of the Peruvian San Pedro by Ross Heaven

Medical Care in Cusco

Eduardo Luna Perez-Ruibal, M.D. has a general practice with a specialty in tourist's needs. He speaks excellent English, has a great bedside manner, and does house/hotel calls for a very reasonable rate.

Cell phone (51) 984-761-277

His office is located at: Calle Umberto Luna #210 in Magisterio, just behind the Real Plaza Mall. Call first for opening hours.

Recommended Reading & Websites, etc.

Masters of the Living Energy: The Mystical World of the Q'ero of Peru
by Joan Parisi Wilcox

The Return of the Inka: A Journey of Initiation & Inka Prophecies
by Elizabeth B. Jenkins

Journey to Q'eros: Golden Cradle of the Inka
by Elizabeth B. Jenkins

The Fourth Level: Nature Wisdom Teachings of the Inka
by Elizabeth B. Jenkins

The Andean Codex: Adventures and Initiations among the Peruvian Shamans
by J. E. Williams

The Light of the Andes: In Search of Shamanic Wisdom in Peru
by J. E. Williams

Serpent of Light: Beyond 2012–The Movement of the Earth's Kundalini and the Rise of the Female Light
by Drunvalo Melchizedek

The Andes for Beginners
by Linda Nordquist

The Incas–The Royal Commentaries of the Inca
by Garcilaso Inca de la Vega, one of the first literate mestizos (part Inca, part Spanish) in the late 1500's

Narrative of the Incas

by Juan de Betanzos, a Spaniard who lived in Peru as Viceroyalty, in 1557

There are several recommendations for books regarding Ayahuasca and Wachuma in the reference section on Plant Spirit Medicines.

****

For photos of the people and places referred to in this book and for information on Lisa McClendon Sims and tours to Peru : www.SpiritualJourneysPeru.com

For information on Elizabeth Jenkins, The Wirracocha Foundation and *Hatun Karpay* trips to Peru : www.Inka-Online.com & www.TheFourthLevel.org

www.ThePathoftheSun.com : here you can gain access to Seti Gershberg's two documentary films: *Q'ero Mystics of Peru* and *Ayahuasca: Nature's Greatest Gift*

For information on Lesley Myburgh, Casa de la Gringa, Wachuma, and Andean Wings Boutique Hotel : www.AnotherPlanetPeru.org

Glossary

Altomisayoq–a high level Andean *paqo* or priest

Apu–Mountain Spirit or God

Ayahuasqero–a shaman who specializes in working with and facilitating ceremonies using the visionary plant spirit medicine made from Ayahuasca, a combination of Amazonian jungle plants

Ayni–sacred reciprocity; the highest principle in the Andean spiritual tradition; an energetic exchange with another being

Campesina/o–a person from the country; a peasant

Chakana–also known as the Andean Cross, an ancient symbol which is representative of the Andean spiritual path; the Andean Tree of Life

Chakaruna–in Quechua the word *chaka* means "bridge" and the word *runa* means "person". A *chakaruna* is a person that bridges people and things to each other.

Ch'aska–star; an invitation from an *apu*

Chicha–a traditional Andean fermented beverage made from corn

Coca—the coca plant, considered in the Andes to be sacred

Colectivo—a small bus or van that goes from one town to another

Comadre—godmother

Compadre—godfather

Combi—a small bus or van within the city

Despacho—a ceremony performed by Andean *paqos*/priests to offer an energetic exchange of *ayni* with the Nature Spirits as an offering of gratitude or supplication for a specific intention. In this ceremony human energies are transmuted, with *hucha* being sent to the *ukhu pacha*, replacing it with *sami*.

Envidia—envy, jealousy

Halpie—the exchange and chewing of coca leaves in a social setting

Hanaq pacha—in the Andean spiritual path, the upper world where the celestial bodies and spirits reside. It is entirely made up of *sami;* represented by the condor

Hatun—great; grand

Hatun Karpay—in the Andean spiritual tradition, the great or grand initiation

Hatun Q'eros–the ceremonial center in the middle of the Q'eros nation

Hucha–heavy, dense energy created by humans through suffering and negative emotions that has not passed through them and has accumulated within them. If not released *hucha* can manifest into disease. *Hucha* belongs in the *ukhu pacha*, the inner world, where it can be utilized by *Pachamama* to create new life.

Inti Tayta–Father Sun; the sun; the expression of the divine masculine

Karpay–literally "irrigation." It is the word used to signify the activation of the Inka seed within a person; an initiation where an energetic transmission is made between *paqos*

Kawsay–life force energy; known in other traditions as Chi or Prana

Kay Pacha–in the Andean Spiritual path, the middle world; the world in which we live; represented by the puma

Khuya–a sacred stone; a power stone that carries *kawsay* and can be used for healing and connecting with the *apus*. Most Andean *mesas* are comprised mostly of *khuyas*. The Quechua translation is "affection."

K'intu–a fan of three coca leaves, symbolizing the trinity of the three worlds in the Andean tradition

Mama Killa–Mother Moon; a representation of the divine feminine

Mama Qocha–a large body of water; the feminine spirit, the mother of all waters

Mamita–literally "little mama," a term of affection

Masintin–harmonious relationship between things that are similar. Part of the divine complements. See *yanantin*

Mesa–literally "table;" a portable altar or sacred bundle of powerful objects carried by *paqos*, usually stones, which is used ceremonially to transmute energies and/or heal

Munay–love and beauty

Ñawi–literally "eye;" these are energetic centers within the body, similar to the concept of chakras, though not identical

Ñust'a–literally "princess." The word used to describe a feminine *apu* or nature energy

Pacha–time and space continuum; world

Pachamama–Mother Earth; Gaia; a feminine divine, sentient being

Pago–same as a *despacho*

Pampamisayoq–a paqo/Andean priest who works primarily with the energies of *Pachamama*

Paqo—an initiate on the Andean spiritual path; an Andean priest

Poq'po—literally "bubble;" the energy field around a person; aura

Q'ero—indigenous people of Peru, thought to be the direct bloodline descendants of the Inka. They are considered by many to have the most pure and traditional customs and shamanic or mystical practices

Q'oyllurit'i (pron. coy-your-ee-tee)—an ancient, sacred festival held annually in glacial range of the Sinakara Valley

Qosqo—literally "navel." The Quechua way of spelling Cusco, the spiritual center of the Inka Empire

Quechua—the official language of the ancient Inka civilization, which is still in use by approximately seven million people in South America

Sami—literally "nectar." Refined, creative energy that flows freely through humans and the cosmos

Seqe—energetic ley lines that emanate from Cusco throughout the Inka Empire. In the Inka Empire there were approximately 350 *wakas* which are located on *seqes*

Serrano—a person from the Sierras/mountains

Soroche—high altitude sickness

Tawantinsuyu–the four quarters of the Inka Empire

Ukhu pacha–in the Andean spiritual tradition–the lower/inner world; the subconscious, represented by the snake. It is a denser world where *hucha*/heavy energy belongs

Ukuku–literally "bear." A mythical man who embodies the spirit of the bear; a human who is the policing authority at *Q'oyllurit'i* festivals

Wachumera/o–a shaman who specializes in working with and facilitating ceremonies using the visionary plant spirit medicine made from Wachuma, also known as the San Pedro cactus.

Waka–a place in nature, usually a rock out-cropping, lake, cave or spring which has become a strong energy vortex and is an excellent place to release *hucha* to the *ukhu pacha*. There are frequently temples or shrines built on top of them. Wakas are located on *seqes*.

Yanantin–two dissimilar things or beings which complement each other; a divine pair–one cannot exist without the other. See *masintin*

About the Author

Lisa McClendon Sims has been coming to Peru since 2005 and has lived in Peru since 2011.

She is a Paqo, Chakaruna and Pampamisayoq in the Andean tradition, and a Fourth Level initiate of the *Hatun Karpay* by Elizabeth Jenkins and Juan Nuñez del Prado. She is also a Reiki Master and a student of A Course in Miracles.

For more information and photos of the people and places referred to in this book please contact Lisa at
www.SpiritualJourneysPeru.com
DovesFlyInMyHeart@gmail.com

Made in the USA
Columbia, SC
07 January 2020

86512787R00143